Flyfishing Structure

I was asked not to name the person to whom this book is dedicated, but you still know who you are, and it is true that a better sporting companion no one could ask for.

Bob Newman

Flyfishing Structure

The Flyfisher's Guide to Reading and Understanding the Water

Foreword by Mark Sosin
Illustrated by Susan Newman

Sycamore Island Books · Boulder, Colorado

Flyfishing Structure:
The Flyfisher's Guide to Reading and Understanding the Water
by Bob Newman

Copyright © 1998 by Bob Newman

ISBN 1-58160-000-3
Printed in the United States of America

Published by Sycamore Island Books, a division of
Paladin Enterprises, Inc., P.O. Box 1307,
Boulder, Colorado 80306, USA.
(303) 443-7250

Direct inquiries and/or orders to the above address.

Publisher's Cataloging-in-Publication:

Newman, Bob, 1958-
    Flyfishing structure : the flyfisher's guide to
reading and understanding the water / Bob Newman ;
foreword by Mark Sosin ; illustrated by Susan Newman. --
1st ed.
    p. cm.
    Includes bibliographical references and index.
    ISBN 1-58160-000-3

    1. Fly fishing. 2. Fishery management.   I. Newman,
Susan, 1958- II. Title.

SH456.N49 1998   799.1'24
                        QBI98-1049

Neither the author nor the publisher assumes
any responsibility for the use or misuse of
information contained in this book.

Illustrated by Susan Newman.

Contents

v

Acknowledgments

This latest book, like my first and fifteenth, is the result of many kind people who went out of their way to share knowledge with me, lend a hand or some valued advice, or honor me with their friendship. Some of their names are Lefty Kreh; Charles Waterman; Dan Blanton; George Misko; Capt. Bramblett Bradham; Capt. Richard Stuhr; Capt. Rodney Smith; Capt. Brian Horsley; Bob Pigott; Dr. Jay; Capt. Doug Jowett; Capt. Bill Gargan; Capt. Les Hill; Capt. Richard Hyland; Capt. Greg Poole; Capt. Steve Lamp; Capt. Gary Taylor; Bob Moore; Court Dixon, Peter Bernsen, and Scott Fraser of Kinsley & Co., Boulder; Brian and Sharon Elder of Wollaston Lake Lodge; Dale Darling and Mark Rayman of St. Vrain Angler; Eric Blais of Front Range Angler; John Mazurkiewicz of Catalyst Marketing Services and Scientific Anglers; Randy Swisher and Bill Dawson of Sage; Steven Fisher, Jon Fisher, and Nicole Fisher of Urban Angler Ltd.; Milton Hanburry of Trek Safaris; Deborah M. Stone and Tess Cunningham of Pineapple Public Relations and the entire staff of The Lodge on Little St. Simons Island; David Bendix of Buccaneer Travel; Doc Thompson; Craig Harris of C.A. Harris (makers of the world-class yet strangely little known Harris Solitude fly reel); Rex Bledsoe of Fly Logic; Steve and Cathy King; Alice and Karel Starek of Gold Lake Mountain Resort; Steve Riley of Bear Advertising; Brian Shipley; Bob Hyde of Peace & Plenty Bonefish Lodge; Barry Crume of Hardy; Levi "Sandbar" Tarr, Clif Hannah, and Kim Hannah of *The Sportfishing Report*; James R. Babb of *Gray's Sporting Journal*; Mike Jones; Bud Zehmer; "Butch" and Kathy King of Wildman Lake Lodge; Mickey and Maggie Greenwood of Blackfire Flyfishing Guest Ranch; R. Peter Van Gytenbeek of *Fly Fishing in Salt Waters*; Jon Ford for the tight edit, Fran Milner for the beautiful design, plus Donna Duvall, Karen Pochert, Barb Beasley,

VII

Elizabeth Barry, Mike Janich, Sheila Conroy Lund, Chris Kuhn, Marilyn Ranson, Dana Rogers, Paula Garber, Cindy Nolting, Allan Bailey, Wanda Bennett, Tim Dyrendahl, Dan Stone, Curtis Carney, Matt Maloney, Matt Orsi, Jeanne Kisker, Cindy Tiger, Tina Mills, Wendy Ann Apps, Ray Lyman, and Tom Laidlaw of Sycamore Island Books; Peter Bercé for the solid copy edit; Tom Earnhardt; Dean Corbisier of Suzuki Marine; Bill Battles of *Fly Fish America*; Marguerite Miles, Mike Heusner, Martin, and Pedro of Belize River Lodge; George Poveromo, Barry Gibson, Rip Cunningham, and Spider Andresen of *Salt Water Sportsman*; Bo Bennett of Kulik Lodge; Duncan Barnes, David E. Petzal, and Mike Toth of *Field & Stream*, Nick Lyons; Doug and Donna Ibbetson of The Boardwalk Wilderness Lodge; Tom Rosenbauer of The Orvis Company; Dennis and Susan Meier of Tanaku Lodge; Jennifer and Lars Olsson; John Rossi Ireland of Hotel Rancho Leonero; Martha Fields of Adventure Marketing; John Duncan and Eric Kraimer of Scott High Performance Fly Rods; James D. Balestrieri of Holland & Holland; Dave and Barbara Foster; Steve Tooker; Betsy Bullard, Abraham Concepción Quiros, Lindor Jimenez, and Hector "Chileno" of the Golfito Sailfish Rancho; Al Maas; Jamie Nelson of Orvis New York; R.M. "Bob" Lee and Mie Hojo of Hunting World; Cesar Cuba of the Beretta Gallery; Ken Wiles; Chuck Ash; Roy and Maria Ventura of Roy's Zancudo Lodge; Tom Clinkenbeard of Elkhorn Fly Rods; Gary Edwards of the Wyoming Flyfishing Connection; Marty Cecil of Elktrout Lodge; Rick Pelow; and Bob Fant, among many others. Thanks also go to country star Randy Travis, who is a down-to-earth gentleman with a man's handshake, for the kind words on another flyfishing book of mine. But six people in particular stand out who deserve special recognition: my wife, my daughter, my mother, my father, Mark Sosin, and Peder Lund.

I know many people who aren't nearly as fortunate as I am.

Author's Note

In this book the reader will occasionally see a reference to a particular brand or model of something or other that has to do with flyfishing. This book was in no way sponsored by any tackle manufacturer whatsoever. When I mention or recommend a certain rod, reel, line, fly, or what have you, it is because that item works for me. It would be most disingenuous of me to write an entire book on structure and then not tell the reader what my experiences with flyfishing tackle have been over the past 30 years. Therefore, if I say that I used a Scott, St. Croix, Orvis, or Sage rod, an Orvis, Fly Logic, Harris, or Ross reel, or a Scientific Anglers line, then I did just that and found that tackle worthy. And if I mention a certain lodge or guide in relation to a certain fish caught, then I caught that fish because of that lodge or guide.

Foreword

Three hot, sultry, oppressive days in August changed my approach to fish behavior forever. Almost three decades ago, Dr. Bob Bachman and I sat shoulder to shoulder in a carefully camouflaged tree blind overlooking Pennsylvania's Spruce Creek watching brown trout feeding below us. He first showed me how to identify individual fish by the pattern of spots on their body. Then we watched these trout disprove most of the common beliefs concerning fish behavior.

Those fussy feeders slurped food all day long in 90-degree heat and bright sun, ferreting out tumbling nymphs on the bottom, rising to take an insect that landed on the water, and sucking down anything at mid-depth. Dr. Bachman began to talk about structure and feeding stations. He called them "seats in a restaurant" and noted that there are always a limited number of seats. In fact, he showed photos of fish taken from the blind a year apart, and the position was so precise that you could superimpose the eyes in the photos.

Identifying structure holds the key to finding and catching fish in any body of water. Whether a species swims continuously in search of food or lies in ambush for its prey, the seats in that restaurant are very specific. It goes beyond simple habitat. Throw in such factors as water levels, tides, water temperature, and even the color of the water and the equation becomes more complex.

Bob Newman not only understands all this, but explains it exceptionally well in *Flyfishing Structure*. It's an extremely important book because it advances the critical aspects of locating your quarry. Once you learn how to put this practical information to work in the field, you will be able to find fish concentrations even in waters you haven't worked before.

Guides and captains stake their business and reputation on producing fish for

 XI

their clients. If you think about it, they probe the same areas day after day, week after week. That's because fish tend to gravitate to the same places. Each area offers a set of conditions that a certain species deems comfortable and favorable in terms of food sources. Even if you removed a trophy fish from a spot, another would take its place within a reasonable period of time.

A dedicated and determined flyfisher, Bob Newman aims *Flyfishing Structure* at light wand aficionados. So be it, but the principles he advances prove equally valid for anglers of every tackle persuasion. When you read the book, you'll be hard pressed to find a situation that Bob didn't cover. If you do happen upon one, it's easy to follow a logical sequence based on what *Flyfishing Structure* teaches to arrive at the correct answer.

I have known Bob for a long time and have followed his career closely. Each article and book he writes raises the bar another notch. *Flyfishing Structure* sits at the top right now, but only for a short time until Bob unveils his next project. He can't help himself. Twenty years of training as a combat-hardened U.S. Marine (now retired) carries over into everything he undertakes. *Semper Fi* goes beyond a simple expression; it represents a way of life that stresses higher and higher levels of excellence. On the flyfishing scene, he's been there and done that. Trust him to lead you to new achievements and greater knowledge. He's done that for me. I enjoyed every page of *Flyfishing Structure*. You will, too.

Mark Sosin
Boca Raton, Florida

Introduction

Fighting a salmon on a broad Alaskan coastal river. (Chuck Ash photo.)

The first time I heard the word structure applied to fishing was back in 1966 in the Everglades. I was standing in the tackle shop at Loxahatchee, having just gotten done gawking at the huge bass the shop had living in a rain barrel on the porch outside the side door, when two anglers walked by discussing the structure they were going to fish that day from their airboat. They were talking about some holes way back in the sawgrass that only airboats could get to, and they seemed quite sure they knew how to get the monster bass they were in search of out of the water hyacinth that lined the hole. They called the noxious weeds *structure*.

This was a curious word to me, and in the coming years I would hear it more and more often. Little did I know that many years later I would find myself writing books and magazine and newspaper articles and columns on structure, and teaching the finer points of structure to flyfishers in fly shops from Madison Avenue to Longmont, Colorado. In some circles the word was used as often in conversation as a politician is economical with the truth, but in others, such as when I would listen to Capt. Bill Gargan speak of cod and pollock tactics from the helm of the *Shamrock III* as we made our way out toward Wooden Ball and Matinicus from Spruce Head Island, it was never structure but rather just plain bottom. (And that's just what it was, too: bottom.)

1

But that was long, long ago, and today it is my job to tell and teach others what others still have told and taught me about flyfishing. Given that, this book is a study of structure and all its intricacies. This structure might include the following:

— An opening in the spartina grass near The Lodge on Little St. Simons Island off the south coast of Georgia
— Pocketwater above Maine's Pond-in-the-River
— Rare fast water on the Upper White Oak River in the North Carolina town of Belgrade
— The cypress stumps of Louisiana's Lake Maurepas
— The flats of the Indian River Lagoon
— Standing timber in San Diego's Otay Lake
— A slightly larger than average rock along the shore near Colorado's Gold Lake Mountain Resort and Spa
— Lily beds on Minnesota's Birch Lake
— The prolific water of a small, fertile pond rimmed in coontail, sedges, and spatterdock at the Blackfire Flyfishing Guest Ranch in New Mexico's Angel Fire
— A seam along the Olympic Peninsula's Sol Duc
— The quiet cove with submerged brush in the one-time gravel pit near my home in Colorado
— A gravel bar in Arizona's Glen Canyon
— A submerged weed bed on Saskatchewan's Wollaston Lake or the Northwest Territories' Kasba Lake
— The kelp beds off La Jolla
— A bonefish flat along Belize's Long Cay
— A small, rocky pool on the Cimarron River
— A chunk of coral near Exuma or South Andros
— A trough in the surf in front of Baja's Hotel Rancho Leonero
— A hand-dug channel leading to Roy's Zancudo Lodge on Costa Rica's Pacific coast
— A granite boulder in New Hampshire's Lake Winnipesaukee
— The marshes of Charleston and Georgia
— A fast chute in Belize's Black Creek
— A rocky outcropping beside the Golfito Sailfish Rancho in Costa Rica
— Riffles in a small stream beside Elktrout Lodge in the Colorado Rockies
— A deep pool near Alaska's Boardwalk Wilderness Lodge
— A patch of sargassum 15 miles off Miami
— Some rough bottom off Matinicus or Nantucket

The pier and boats of the Golfito Sailfish Rancho on Costa Rica's Pacific coast act as excellent structure.

A hefty cut-throat trout taken in a ranch pond at Colorado's Elktrout Lodge. (Marty Cecil photo.)

This book was written because virtually every species of gamefish in the world depends one way or another upon structure for its existence. Black marlin use structure just as readily as bluegill, but in different ways. The same can be said of rock bass and steelhead, brown trout and tarpon, red drum and tripletail, northern pike and smallmouth bass, trevally and orange-mouth corvina, and all other gamefish.

In a recent interview I was asked what knowledge is perhaps the most important a flyfisher could have. I answered that knowledge of the water's structure would rate highly, but it would have to be coupled with a knowledge of what gamefish in that water feed on and how they feed on it. Therefore, here you will find tactics and techniques that cover every imaginable situation as they pertain to structure in lakes, ponds, rivers, streams, creeks, reservoirs, gravel pits, quarries, and tailwaters, as well as that found inshore and offshore.

What you won't find is someone preaching to you about how much money you should spend on tackle and whether or not you should be allowed to keep the occasional fish for supper. Whereas I release nearly all of the fish I catch, and whereas all my fly rods are graphite and some of my reels are somewhat pricey, I see nothing wrong with keeping a trout from time to time if doing so in no way injures the fishery, and I have the aforementioned tackle only because I find that it helps me catch more fish. Here you will not be chastised if you use inexpensive tackle and eat a fish once in a while.

This may not sit well with the well-known flyfishing writer who lives in the town just west of mine—a writer with several book credits and a column in a major fishing and hunting magazine. He recently went out of his way in a column in the local newspaper to sideswipe an elderly gentleman whom he ran into on a stream in Wyoming recently and who used a "fiberglass rod" and an "automatic reel" to take home "three dead trout." Such unbridled arrogance is the parlance of the elitist parvenu. I hope never to be so consumed by the fires of my own self-importance.

So let's wade right in and start off by visiting some nice neighborhoods.

4

Chapter 1

Neighborhoods

Cabo San Lucas harbor, one of the busiest sport-fishing ports in the world and a perfect neighbor-hood for a variety of gamefish.

Walking down the broad, vendor-infested esplanade that lines the barely controlled pandemonium that is Cabo San Lucas harbor, a 25-pound yellowfin tuna in one hand and a 9-weight rod in the other, I was struck not only by the throbbing port's remarkable number of boats but by the number of fish that live everywhere in and around the harbor. With me was a 16-year veteran of Cabo, Grant Hartman, owner of Baja Anglers, the top flyfishing charter service in the Baja boomtown, who runs a brace of custom-rigged Glacier Bay SeaCat catamarans designed with the flyfisher in mind.

"Bob, look at the cubera," he said, pointing at the shadowy form of a big snapper hovering in the shade beneath a yacht-lined quay. "Come down in the morning right at dawn before it gets too hot and you can hook that fish."

"How am I supposed to keep him away from the pilings, props, and rocks?" I asked, looking at the heavy structure everywhere and within a few feet of the handsome snapper.

"You probably can't. That's the challenge. You'll need to put the rod to him hard and turn him as soon as he eats your fly. Use your 12-weight. Heavy shock tippet. They've got serious teeth," the master flyfishing guide replied.

*The author
with a Cabo
yellowfin.*

"Mmm," I said, remembering the first cubera I ever saw. It was a big fish taken off Ft. Lauderdale back in 1967, and I can still picture the teeth it used to hunt lobster and other taste treats, mostly at night.

Taking in the busy port again—there were hundreds of boats of all shapes and sizes plying the dark blue waters, from a spectacular 130-foot sailing yacht to colorful and simple *pangas*—I asked Grant how it was that such impressive and worthy gamefish as the apparently snoozing cubera came to stay in such a raucous environment.

"It's their neighborhood. They have everything they need right where they are," came the matter-of-fact reply.

It's their neighborhood. Yes, I thought to myself, *fish live in neighborhoods.*

FISH IN THE 'HOOD

Fish live in neighborhoods, many of which don't appear at first glance to be the most hospitable place to call home. But consider the Iowa hog farmer who flips on the set after a hard day on the farm and watches a television show about life in the Bronx, Chicago's South Side, East St. Louis, or the Overtown area of Miami. He may very well think that such places are uninhabitable, with rampant crime, gang warfare, and people packed into cramped hovels with bars on the windows that they call home. Still, most of the folks living in these places wouldn't consider the farmer's spread in Iowa to be an option, either. The people in each kind of place live in their own niche and have adapted to life there, just as that brutish cubera has adapted to life beneath a dock in one of the busiest recreational angling ports in the world. Just as the farmer has had to adapt to long, cold winters and broiling summers, and the city folks have had to adapt to dense populations and an astounding crime rate amid the decay of the city, so the cubera has had to adapt to the myriad buzzing boats and human feet stomping on his dock. He lives there because what he needs is there. It is his neighborhood, and he isn't likely to leave any time soon. Nor, do I suspect, is he likely to be caught.

Foundation

Structure forms the foundation of the fish's neighborhood, and from this foundation all else comes. Water temperature, barometric pressure and other weather changes, forage availability, currents, visibility, and all other factors affecting the behavior of gamefish revolve around structure, from bluegill to blue marlin, trout to tuna, carp to crappie. The flyfisher who can find and read structure is far along the path to catching the gamefish living on or in close association with that structure.

But just what is structure?

Structure is anything within the water column other than the fish and water itself, including changes in the bottom. Examples of structure include the following:

- A mat, or even a single piece, of sargassum
- Rocks forming pocketwater or lies in general in a stream or river
- A slight depression in a streambed adjacent to Alaska's Tanaku Lodge
- A former Navy destroyer, now intentionally retired to rest forever on the sea floor
- The chains and anchor of a buoy, and the buoy itself
- A rock on an otherwise unremarkable bottom

A mainstay fly like the Lefty's Deceiver, created by Lefty Kreh, imitates many species and is a great structure-prospecting fly.

7

- Fallen trees lining a lake's shoreline
- A coral reef
- A shoal covered with seaweed and exposed at low tide
- Milfoil
- A two-by-four or truck tire floating on the surface
- A lobster pot off Marblehead, Massachusetts
- Coontail
- A rocky river bank near Kulik Lodge in Alaska
- A granite ledge
- A scallop dragger that went down off Isle au Haut in 1975
- A cable running through Hanauma Bay or an old landing craft off Kaho'olawe
- Discarded 55-gallon drums and steel pipes piled on the bottom
- Pondweed
- A DC-3 formerly used by a drug smuggler now sitting in 80 feet of water
- A sudden rise in the sea floor
- Pickerelweed
- A crab pot in Louisiana's Owl Bayou
- A culvert
- A swing-bridge abutment over the Banana River Lagoon
- A sudden drop-off along the banks of south Georgia's Altamaha River
- Anything else that is either natural or provided by man, intentionally or otherwise, which now holds or attracts gamefish

What all structure has in common, regardless of where it came from and when it got there, is its ability to create homes and forage for fish. So, the sunken Japanese warships in Truk Lagoon and sunken shore batteries below the cliffs on the Mokapu Peninsula are structure, just as the Monterey kelp beds and San Diego bait barges (floating baitfish pens) are structure. The same holds true for granite boulders in Maine's Pocomoonshine Lake, a log on Brazil's Rio Negro, deep in the Amazon basin, where the *Amazon Queen* searches for peacock bass, and mangrove roots in a narrow canal on Florida's Sanibel Island. If it is something other than a flat, barren bottom that fish gravitate toward or live in or on—besides the water itself and the fish themselves—it is structure.

Once the foundation of structure is formed, whether this foundation comes in the shape of a Spanish galleon filled with looted Central American treasure sunk in a hurricane off the Tortugas, a red pine toppling into Minnesota's Birch Lake, dock pilings on North Carolina's Neuse River, or fresh lava rolling down the slopes of Kilauea to meet the sea in a mesmerizing spectacle of steam, molten rock, and ocean, a neighborhood is born. In most cases, life establishes itself in or on the new structure in a surprisingly short time, and might include

- some frilled, silver-spotted, or club-tipped sea anemones;
- crayfish;
- hydroids like the bushy wine-glass, solitary, and tropical garland;
- some yellow perch;
- red, curly, and pale terebellid worms;
- tube and loggerhead sponges;
- sea fans;
- fathead minnows;
- a great barracuda;
- sea whips;
- a smallmouth bass;
- a school of spadefish;
- colonial tunicates and sea squirts;
- a landlocked salmon;
- giant feather duster and spiral-gilled tube worms;
- a flathead catfish;
- assorted coral polyps;
- a moray eel;
- sea hares; and
- an unending array of other life.

Sometimes a handful of flies will suffice (above), but other times you will need a more extensive repertoire (left).

But simply knowing where the structure is, and knowing precisely what that structure is—even if you can't see it, as in the case of a sunken vessel—does not mean your fly will be readily inhaled by a waiting fish. The flyfisher must know far more. The flyfisher must know what species has made the structure home—who has moved into the

Below: A Gold Lake rainbow approaches and eats Scott Fraser's ant.

Top right: Excellent sunglasses, such as these Costa Del Mar shades worn by Kinsley & Company's Court Dixon, are crucial for seeing subsurface structure.

Right: Steve King and Elktrout's Marty Cecil admire the results of reading and understanding the water.

neighborhood—and what factors affect that species' behavior when, how, and why. He must also have the right flies available when they are needed, and then know how to use them.

Let's begin with an examination of saltwater surface structure—man-made and that which nature provides.

Chapter 2

Saltwater Surface Structure

A commercial fishing boat ironically acts as saltwater surface structure.

For our purposes, let's consider saltwater surface structure as that structure actually on or very near the surface, such as within a few feet. Saltwater surface structure runs the gamut from flotsam and jetsam to aquatic algae like sargassum, as well as docks, shallow oyster beds, boats, jetties, bait barges, the uppermost portion of kelp, and pieces or mats of gulfweed and rockweed that have broken loose from their rocks.

I am continually struck by the diversity of surface structure in salt water and am astounded by the proliferation of life that can take place when conditions are right. The flyfisher must be prepared to fish a variety of types of surface structure. One of the most magnificent insofar as diversity and a plethora of life is a healthy kelp bed.

KELP BEDS

I first fully experienced a kelp bed many years ago off San Clemente Island, a semi-arid piece of real estate owned by the U.S. Navy that is the southernmost island in the Channel Islands forming the southern end of the Outer Santa Barbara Passage. The waters immediately surrounding San Clemente are off limits to most because of the military activity that goes on there—things like diving operations and the training of Navy SEALs and sailors trying to become SEALs. I was in the

Marines at the time, and one of the skills required of my job in reconnaissance was scuba diving.

Rolling backward off the side of the Zodiac inflatable boat, I slowly descended with my dive partner, Ron Wendt, through the cold (52 degrees) November water to the rocky bottom in a gentle free fall. On the way down amid the giant olive drab kelp trees that gently swayed back and forth in the current, I was fascinated with the number and variety of fish going about their lives.

The entire water column was alive. Just below the surface were Pacific barracuda (smaller, much less ferocious relatives of the mighty great barracuda of the Atlantic and Caribbean), California needlefish, Pacific bonito (racing by in the open water just beyond the edge of the kelp forest), California yellowtail, white seabass, anchovies (there are five species that inhabit those waters), frogfish (cleverly camouflaged to appear as just another piece of kelp), and seemingly countless other species of baitfish that I couldn't recognize because of their fleeting nature.

In the middle layer of the water column there

Above: Ken Wiles with a North Carolina dolphin found in scattered sargassum.

Right: Brightly colored poppers draw strikes from many species, ranging from amberjack and dolphin to cobia and barracuda.

were more white seabass and the beginnings of the kelp bass (also called calico bass, they are relatives of the sand bass, which are much smaller), a popular, hard-hitting gamefish that far too few flyfishers target with any degree of seriousness and which grow to nearly 15 pounds. Nearing and then standing on the bottom as I adjusted my buoyancy compensator (an inflatable vest used to adjust one's buoyancy while diving), I could see great schools of California sheephead (an often large and always delicious red, black, and white member of the wrasse family), dainty Garibaldis (a type of damselfish) dressed in their coats of brilliant orange, a strange horn shark lying absolutely still on the bottom (a small, quite docile shark with a face like a pig), some juvenile canary rockfish, a giant cabezon (a kind of overgrown sculpin) that appeared to weigh more than 20 pounds, and innumerable other species.

The sea floor was alive with creatures of all kinds. There were well-camouflaged abalone and other mollusks of many shapes, colors, and sizes (wavy turbans, dogwinkles, thorn drupes, and top shells, to name a few), California moray eels, spiny lobsters, crabs, searobins, brightly painted gobies, and huge numbers of sea urchins and sea anemones. It reminded me very much of a temperate forest in spring, with life everywhere and at all levels. Although I was enjoying the dive immensely, I was now all the more anxious to return to the surface and our dive boat so that I could decompress and cast flies at the same time.

The Kelp Bed's Upper Reaches

Flyfishers in California kelp beds will find Pacific barracuda and bonito two of the most common gamefish near the surface. Feeding primarily on anchovies and sardines, these two very different fish are equals in their own right, hitting hard and giving a good show of themselves. Particularly in the case of the barracuda, which can weigh nearly 8 pounds and grow to more than 3 feet, the flyfisher is often treated to a thrilling charge from an irate 'cuda similar to that made by its overgrown cousin in the temperate and subtropical waters of the Atlantic and Caribbean. The barracuda can be best provoked into an attack by tossing several lively anchovies into a small opening in the kelp along with a dead one or two and some smaller chunks to give the appearance of a massacre in progress. When the nearby 'cudas see, hear, and feel the anchovies hitting the water and scattering, they tend to attack without much thought or adieu whatsoever. As soon as the first fish charges, cast a fly that imitates the anchovies into the melee, such as a dark green and gray 2/0 to 4/0 Deceiver with some Flashabou, Mylar, or Krystal Flash tied into it. Try to make the fly slap the water hard to add to the fracas.

As soon as the fly hits the water, begin a fast and erratic retrieve so that the fly acts just as the anchovies do. (Although an anchovy certainly does not enjoy cognizant thought, it does have the instinct of a baitfish and knows that it is in tremendous peril the moment it hits the water, so it flees the second it hits the surface. Your fly should act the same way.) It is important in this situation not to attempt to set the hook the moment it appears that the barracuda has hit your fly. Instead, wait until you feel some pressure and then strip-strike the fish. Keep your rod tip low to the water and the rod pointed directly at the fly.

The bonito in the kelp (especially just along the outside edge in or near the open water) can be caught in a similar fashion as dolphin (mahi mahi, dorado). This is done by trolling a bonito feather on heavy spinning or medium trolling gear (medium to heavy gear is best because these fish are hard fighters that weigh up to 20 pounds and then some, and the angler needs to bring the fish to the boat quickly before the rest of the school scatters) at 7 to 10 knots; bonito belong to the tuna family and therefore are powerful swimmers that have no problem catching something swimming at such speeds. When one is hooked it is brought to the boat, and as soon as it is within fly-casting range, send a fly such as the aforementioned Deceiver its way. Several members of the school, and sometimes the entire school, will follow the first bonito as it is reeled in and will willingly eat flies cast toward them.

California yellowtail have legions of followers in southern California, and with good reason: they are powerful fighters and can grow to about 80 pounds, although they average about 15 pounds, with 30- and 40-pound fish being regularly reported, especially in the Coronado Islands, which lie in Mexican waters. A type of amberjack actually, many if not most are broken off quickly as the bullish fish rampages through the kelp and wraps the unprepared flyfisher's leader around the stout kelp trunks. However, shock tippets of between 50- and 80-pound test and rugged leaders will prevent many break-offs. The same tactics used for the Pacific barracuda will work on yellowtail, but instead of an 8- to 10-weight rod, a 12-weight is used to better cast large flies (up to 5/0) and deal with the ornery and stubborn yellowtail.

With powerful fish such as these, it is important to apply as much pressure to the fish as you feel you can get away with. To wear a fish down faster, apply pressure in the opposite direction it is running in. If it is bearing to the left, flip the rod to your right and apply side pressure, and vice versa. This technique will tire the fish much faster than if you go with the flow by putting left pressure on a fish bearing to the left, likewise to a fish bearing to the right.

SARGASSUM

As a boy I recall reading about the mysterious Sargasso Sea, a place somewhere in the Atlantic Ocean where currents formed a dead zone filled with seaweed known as sargassum. It was said to be littered with ghost ships that had

14

become stranded in the mire of oceanic algae, and I seem to remember my hero, Jonny Quest, along with his father Dr. Quest, Race Bannon (their hired gun), Jonny's friend Hadji, and their dog Bandit, having an adventure there. It was also said that the American eel, that slimy, repulsive fish occasionally caught on worms fished on the bottom, migrated from their homes in the lakes, ponds, and rivers of the eastern United States and Canada to the Sargasso Sea to give birth to all the young eels, which were alleged to be transparent.

I would learn later in life that the part about the Sargasso Sea being strewn with becalmed ghost ships was somewhat less than accurate, but on the other hand I found that Dr. Johannes Schmidt, in the early 20th century, discovered that, yes, the American eel does indeed travel to the Sargasso Sea to give birth to tremendous numbers of transparent eels, the strange newborn eel being called a leptocephalus. The baby eels would then begin their incredible year-long migration toward the eastern shore of North America, transforming on the way until they finally looked like the well-known American eel about the time they reached the littorals.

Wherever sargassum really comes from, flyfishers take great pleasure in finding and casting flies at mats of the dull green algae because of its wonderful ability to attract small fish, which in turn attract larger fish, which in turn attract people like you and me.

Sargassum is found in both the Northern and Southern Hemispheres and is especially common from the mid-Atlantic to the Caribbean and into the Gulf of Mexico. It drifts with the prevailing currents and winds, often carrying with it tiny sea creatures that get the attention of filefish, puffers, members of the boxfish family, small queen triggerfish, and that master of intricate camouflage, the sargassumfish. These draw dolphin, tripletail, cobia, and other popular gamefish. Consequently, the big boys like tuna, king mackerel, wahoo, and billfish come to patrol areas with sargassum floating about to prey upon the small dolphin (sometimes called yellowjackets) and tripletail (if they can be seen; their camouflage is also excellent, whereas a dolphin's isn't).

Joe Slappey with a yellow-jacket dolphin that fell for the right approach beside a sargassum mat.

There are three primary techniques for approaching sargassum (and don't think that gamefish need large mats of the stuff before considering it a good hunting ground; small pieces widely scattered can hold surprising numbers of gamefish), and it was *Salt Water Sportsman*'s George Poveromo who first lumped the three techniques together into a practical game plan for effectively working dolphin around sargassum: trolling, running and gunning, and chumming and chunking.

Trolling

First, do not be put off by the word *trolling* appearing in a flyfishing book. In this instance, just as in this chapter's section on Pacific bonito near a kelp bed, trolling is simply an effective means of finding gamefish that, at the moment, can't be readily located by casting flies. In many situations, trolling can be an outstanding technique for finding cruising gamefish that otherwise would go unmolested by the flyfisher.

When trolling near sargassum, it is critical to do so with tackle heavy enough to withstand the power and size of serious gamefish such as sailfish, wahoo, tuna,

and marlin, even though you are looking for dolphin. These brutes inhabit the same waters as dolphin and are commonly caught by anglers trolling baits intended for dolphin. Heavy gear will give you a better chance of boating the invader and will also improve your chances of getting a crazed and hefty bull dolphin near enough to the boat for flies to be cast at the other dolphin that come with it as it approaches the boat. Monofilament in the 80-pound-test range and steel leaders used with stout rods and reels that can put serious pressure on the fish are required.

Once a dolphin crashes the trolled baits, strikes one, and is solidly hooked, the other lines are brought in quickly and stowed. Fly lines are now stripped onto the deck so that they are free and unfouled, the flyfishers manning the fly rods ready to cast with double hauls if necessary once the dolphin buzzing around the hooked fish come into casting range. As the action gets serious with multiple hook-ups, one dolphin is always left in the water as others are released or brought aboard. This technique keeps the dolphin around the boat longer, resulting in more hook-ups.

The author found this wahoo mixed in with dolphin; a pleasant albeit alarming surprise.

Running and Gunning

Running and gunning involves flyfishers' moving rapidly in between sargassum mats or areas with small patches of dispersed sargassum in search of fish. When a mat or other area of sargassum is approached, the boat is slowed some distance away so that any fish lurking in the area aren't spooked. Binoculars (Tasco's Offshore 54 model is excellent) and sharp eyes look for signs of feeding gamefish or gamefish hiding beneath mats. They are also looking right underneath the mats to see whether there are any small fish that could be forage for gamefish. Mats with no baitfish seldom hold good numbers of gamefish.

If baitfish or the real thing are seen, flies are cast in searching patterns—casts meant to cover as much likely looking water in the least amount of time. If two flyfishers are casting, each should have on different flies, such as a gold-and-

16

brown Clouser Deep Minnow and a red-and-white Deceiver, or any other diverse patterns that mimic two different baitfish or other forage, such as crabs and shrimp. When a fish hits, the other flyfisher quickly switches to that fly pattern and continues casting.

The keys to running and gunning are

- finding sargassum (made easier by working the radio and using binoculars),
- determining whether the sargassum holds baitfish or observable gamefish,
- covering as much good-looking water as possible in a short period, and
- using fly search patterns to ascertain what the gamefish are interested in.

Chumming and Chunking

Most flyfishers find chumming and chunking to be the most exciting approach because of the way frenzies tend to get going at close quarters—and the fish you are targeting are done so by sight-casting, which is always a thrill, especially when the fish are rambunctious and some real bruisers are seen amid the mayhem. But there is a lot more to it than just tossing in handfuls of ground-up fish.

Chumming and chunking is best done with a controlled plan in mind. Begin with a frozen chum block suspended in a mesh bag several feet beneath the boat so that the chum drifts toward the sargassum (an often missed point), where the baitfish are hiding. As the frozen chum defrosts, small baitfish are attracted to it and begin to feed on the pieces that reach them. They will soon get up the courage to leave the safety of their mat and wander closer to the block itself as their interest is piqued. As the baitfish gather, gamefish will begin to take note. Small chunks of half handfuls of chum are intermittently tossed into the water where the chum is spreading toward the sargassum. Gamefish seeing these chunks

will often become antsy and move in to get a quick bite. As they do, a few live baitfish from the live well are tossed in amid the chunks and chum line to really get the gamefish fired up.

Flies can be cast at any time in this process, but the mistake of adding too much chum and too many chunks (and live bait) to the equation must be avoided. You want to entice and excite the gamefish, not give them a free feast.

Watch to see how deep the chunks and baitfish sink or swim before the gamefish attack, and then time your cast to coincide with the chunks' and bait-

Fresh baitfish like pinfish and menhaden make good chum.

A large yellow or chartreuse popper causing commotion in a chum slick can cause dolphin to throw all caution to the wind.

Baitfish moving along the surface.

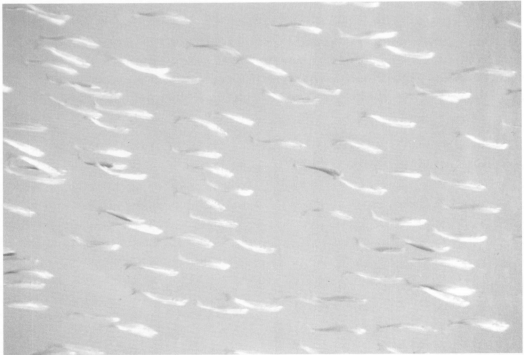

18

fishes' hitting the water. Put the fly right in the middle of it all and allow it to sink to the depth the fish are feeding at before beginning your retrieve. Weighted flies can come in handy and even be crucial, as can sink-tip and full-sink lines of various grains.

Pay attention to what flies are working best and stick with them until the action slows, then change. Be watchful for fish turning off entirely or making false runs at bait and flies. When this happens you must switch flies or try different retrieves and presentations, such as using a Judas stick to swat the surface (giving the fish the impression that someone is feeding aggressively and that they should do the same) or switching from a subsurface presentation to one on the surface that tells the fish a wounded victim is nearby and is easy prey. A fly rod rigged with a loud, splashy popper will sometimes turn fish back on, although the school just as often becomes reinvigorated for only a short time. Sometimes all it takes to get the fish turned back on is a different color of fly being presented, even though the pattern is identical to the one you were casting in all other respects.

COLOR CHANGES

Although not structure per se, color changes of surface water, which can be caused by two currents colliding (often of different temperature) or which might delineate the blue water of the open ocean from the green, near-shore water, are to be given attention. These color changes can act like seams in a trout stream and often hold gamefish on the prowl, such as dolphin, cobia, tripletail, and false albacore.

Regardless of where you find a color change, fish it. Explore the surface and on down to perhaps 15 feet with a sink-tip. Work both the blue and green side. Vary the speed of your strips and other aspects of your presentation. When you see a bit of weed or any other apparently insignificant piece of structure, work it and the water around it hard.

FLOTSAM, JETSAM, AND DEBRIS IN GENERAL

While fishing a few hundred yards off the beach between North Carolina's New River Inlet and Bogue Inlet one day, I spotted three gulls sitting in the water, with few other sea birds anywhere about. Turning the boat toward them, I slowed and scanned the water around them with my binos.

Sure enough, what I suspected was there, was there—a sea turtle was snoozing in the morning sun. Quietly edging my way toward the turtle and birds, I cut the motor just as I came into casting range and worked a 2/0 Bramblett's Swimming Shrimp (the phenomenal creation of Hilton Head's Captain Bramblett

Even sea turtles can act as structure. (U.S. Marine Corps photo.)

Bradham) out toward the turtle and let it hit the water about six feet away without disturbing the birds or their benefactor. Immediately I saw the shadowy form of a tripletail leave the shade beneath the turtle and casually drift toward the fly, pretending to be just another piece of whatever in the water. When it got within a foot of the fly it attacked—the fight was on!

I had seen many tripletail do this sort of thing and laughed the whole fight through—until it broke me off at the side of the boat just as I reached for the net, a most disconcerting turn of events. Even more annoying was the way the fish just swam back to its shade beneath the turtle and refused to come out again.

No, that turtle wasn't flotsam, jetsam, or debris, but the point is made: anything floating on the surface can and often will attract gamefish, and there is a lot more junk floating about than sea turtles.

An Eclectic Selection

Gamefish such as dolphin, tripletail, greater amberjack, and cobia are all drawn to nearly any floating object in the water. Tires, boards, plastic bags, coolers, hats, tarps—you name it and they can be attracted to it. They will even be drawn to a boat if the anglers inside stay quiet enough. Always check anything seen floating in the water.

Palm fronds and coconuts are the predominant surface structure in the Golfo Dulce region near Golfito and Zancudo, Costa Rica. This large bay is

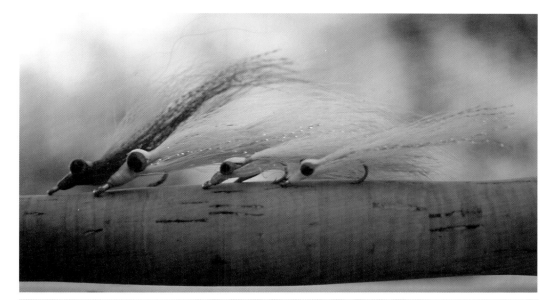

Clouser Deep Minnows.

Poppers.

21

teeming with more Pacific bonito than you could ever hope for, not to mention bigeye trevally, roosterfish, cubera snapper, leatherjackets (oftentimes seen in feeding frenzies that boggle the mind and put to shame even the most hideous bluefish bloodfest), sierras, Pacific dogtooth snapper, Pacific crevalle jack (great swarms of the things, many of which are clearly IGFA record contenders; see Roy Ventura at his gorgeous Zancudo Lodge if you would like to own such a record), and other gamefish. However, the surface structure here is rather unimportant to the bonito, the numbers of which can be best appreciated from the air; a plane ride over the Golfo Dulce in March of 1998 after spending some time at the famous Golfito Sailfish Rancho (recently purchased and reopened by Betsy Bullard and Abraham Concepción Quiros) and the aforementioned Roy's Zancudo Lodge (if you haven't fished with Roy, you have yet to experience the true meaning of the word fanatical) showed me dozens of schools of hungry bonito frantically attacking herring and other baitfish from one end of the bay to the other. They were feeding frenzies that you dream about, and the little tunas were happy to attack nearly any fly presented to them.

Although the bonito are feeding voraciously, to get at them on the surface close enough to present a fly you must approach them slowly and quietly and have your double haul ready to go with at least 40 feet of line piled up in large, loose coils at your feet. Our captain at the Sailfish Rancho, Lindor Jimenez, who has been a sportfishing captain in the region for 15 years, is an expert at sneaking up on the bonito before they get suspicious and disappear. Also, make sure your reel's drag is smooth and consistent with a flawless startup, because bonito will run and bolt and

A typical Pacific bonito taken while flyfishing at the Golfito Sailfish Rancho. The reel is a Fly Logic.

run again and again. A drag like that of a Harris Solitude (a very good reel that is really getting noticed because of its Teflon and cork disk drag), Scientific Anglers System 2, Orvis Battenkill, Ross Gunnison, or Fly Logic is needed.

Offshore, the effects of there being so many bonito available become obvious. Here sailfish abound, and any flyfisher who doesn't partake of this astound-

The teasers are laid out on the transom. (Peder Lund photo.)

Peder Lund does battle with his first sailfish on the fly. Note that he quickly learned to bow to the fish when it jumped.

The author with a beautiful sail-fish courtesy of Lindor and Hector. (Peder Lund photo.)

Ready for release.

ing action is a kook who should have his rods taken away. The Golfito Sailfish Rancho and Roy's Zancudo Lodge are the two top operations in the region that target sails on the fly, and they do it with style. On a calm day in the winter of 1998, the surface as flat as a mill pond, Lindor and Hector "Chileno" of the Sailfish Rancho took Peder Lund and me offshore to show us how exciting Pacific sails on a fly can be. Although we saw several basking on the surface and went after them, the teasers we were dragging went ignored. The sails we did catch all showed up in the spread unannounced and were very angry by the time they were at the stern of the boat, the teasers having been pulled away by Lindor and Hector. We could have touched each sail with the tips of our rods, they were so close. The flashy Curcione's Big Game Fly (well-known fly-tier and flyfishing author Nick Curcione's creation) went just behind and beside each sail as it frantically searched for something to attack and eat, and each immediately assaulted the fly as soon as it saw it. The 15-weight, 8 1/2-foot rods, Billy Pate tarpon reels, and 16-pound tippets were the order of the day, and no sail threw the fly or broke off. This was saltwater surface action at its finest.

Freshwater structure is just as intricate as saltwater structure. Let's have a peek.

25

Chapter 3

Freshwater Surface Structure

Thick mixtures of weeds near the surface of fresh-water bodies of water can hide surprising num-bers of fish.

Recently I was in my float tube on McCall Reservoir, which is between Lyons and Longmont, Colorado, a few miles east of the foothills of the Rocky Mountains, and about 40 minutes north of Denver. This small water has quite a bit of structure, with fallen trees, coontail (*Ceratophyllum*), rocks, spatterdock (*Nuphar luteum*; also known as yellow pondlily), and other types of cover available to the warm-water species like bass and bream living there. However, soon after I put in I was surrounded by dozens of bream that followed me all along the shoreline. They were using me as struc-ture, abandoning their static structure for that which was moving from place to place and kicking up assorted tiny creatures, which they promptly devoured. But flyfishers in float tubes aren't the only kind of freshwater structure.

Pondweed (*Potamogeton illinoensis*), great bulrush (*Scirpus validus*), that portion of a dock away from the shore, floats, boats, cattails (*Typha latifolia* and *Typha angustifolia*), pickerelweed (*Pontederia cordata*), coontail, Eurasian water milfoil (*Myriophyllum spicatum*, an often troublesome 19th-century import that may have arrived in North America as an aquarium plant or in the ballast of ships), waterlily (*Nymphaea*), pondlily (*Nuphar*), lotus (*Nelumbo*), water hyacinth (*Eichhornia crassipes*, a nasty South American import) duckweed (*Lemna*), blad-

*The log and
brush that hid
Blackface.*

Blackface.

derwort (primarily *Utricularia vulgaris* and *Utricularia inflata*), and anything
else on or near the surface of fresh water is surface structure, and that structure
can be and often is just as intricate as that found in salt water. In a former gravel
pit near my home, now called Webster Pond, which is filled with largemouth that
are apparently completely unafraid of intruders like my deranged Labrador, Rocky

the Bird Swallower, structure exists in the form of standing and fallen timber; brush; cattails; spatterdock; small rock and gravel islands; assorted banks made of rocks, sand, dirt, and mud; and various types of emergent vegetation breaking and completely below the surface, some in holes 10 feet deep very close to shore. A diverse little pond that is heavily fished. (I could swim across it in about three minutes; I am a strong swimmer as a result of spending three years training life-guards in the Marines in Southern California. Why, yes, as a matter of fact, that was a great scam. Your tax dollars at work.)

Recently I was in the middle of a very educational session (I was the student, I assure you) with some bass, one of which has an apparent birthmark on the right side of its head (see photo on page 28). The surface of the pond was alive with bass feeding on egg-laying dragonflies (mostly western widows, white-tailed skimmers, and biddies) and any glance would take in no fewer than 10 strikes on the surface. I was standing between two fallen trees on a gentle gravel bank that had the remnants of numerous bass beds recently abandoned by the now post-spawn bass, and a few bream were still on their nests in the same area. Some spatterdock was scattered here and there.

After catching 20 or so small bass, none heavier than a pound (most were hitting absolutely still presentations of small Muddler Minnows about eight inches below the surface), an obviously larger female appeared in the shallow, clear water in front of me cruising the shoreline. I had just tied on a Joe's Hopper and cast the fly about 10 feet in front of her. She quickly swam forward and took the fly in a quick but fairly soft gulp.

I set the hook and the fight was on, the fat bass thrashing and shaking her head on the surface. A couple of seconds into the fight a second bass, this one slightly smaller, rushed out from beneath the log and brush on my right and frantically pursued the bass I had hooked through every twist and turn, never getting more than a few inches away. The curious bass was the one with the birthmark, and I was surprised to see the bass come right up to my feet and stop as I lipped the fat female, removed the fly, and released her. Blackface was still there in a foot of water and he didn't move from that spot, even as I released the other bass, which quickly swam out to some moss in about 6 feet of water to sulk.

Blackface began patrolling back and forth along the bank. I flipped the fly back out and was quickly rewarded with a strike from a young bass about 8 inches long. Blackface turned sharply and attacked, closing the distance of 15 feet in a heartbeat. His mouth opened and he slammed into the little bass with considerable force.

My 5-weight rod bent mightily under the strain of what was now two bass, but I knew Blackface wasn't hooked and was rather just being stubborn in not letting go of the smaller bass. For 10 seconds I fought them both until finally Blackface let go and I stripped the battered little bass in. I removed the fly and

released the fish, which got only 4 feet from the bank before Blackface pounced with gusto. Blackface caught the hapless young bass sideways and drove it into the bottom repeatedly until it was sufficiently stunned, at which time he swallowed it whole in one shuddering gulp. All the while I was looking around trying to find someone to witness these events with me, but no one was there.

Blackface resumed his constant patrol of the bank and only once showed an interest in my flies, but he spit the fly out just as quickly as he inhaled it, and my strike was to no avail.

But what role did structure play in all this? Structure attracted and held all the fish I caught (and tried to catch). The fallen trees, gentle gravel bank, spatterdock, and moss all played their respective parts, and the clear water and pleasant Rocky Mountain sun (it was 95 degrees) merely added to the equation in providing excellent visibility. The dragonflies were cooperating, too, making many of the bass anxious and rambunctious. Fortunately, I have been flyfishing for about 30 years and was able to put the pieces of the puzzle together after a while.

But what about Blackface? Why was he only interested in eating other bass and not the plethora of dragonflies dropping eggs all over the pond? I mean frankly, he appeared to be almost absolutely disinterested in what all the other bass were doing and only wanted to eat what were certainly his offspring and their neighbors.

Such is flyfishing, and I only wish I had an answer for you.

DIVERSITY

Freshwater structure can be even more diverse than saltwater structure. I recently returned to my home in Colorado from northern Minnesota, where I spend a week or so every summer casting flies to musky, northern pike, largemouth and smallmouth bass, panfish, and the occasional bowfin. The bowfin is, in my opinion, the most underrated freshwater gamefish in North America. Comprising a single member in the *Amiidae* family, this ancient fish from the Jurassic is found in the Northeast and the Southeast, throughout the Deep South, and into the Midwest at least as far north as northern Minnesota. It inhabits lakes, ponds, canals, swamps, sloughs, backwaters, slow-moving rivers and streams, bayous, and the Everglades, almost always near or in aquatic vegetation of some kind such as water hyacinth, lily pads, and sawgrass. I have caught them from Minnesota's lakes region (where they are known as dogfish) to Owl Bayou in Louisiana (where they are called *choupique*; pronounced "shoe pick") and the Everglades' Loxahatchee region (where the local name is mudfish). A hard-hitting fish, the bowfin or grinnel has a gas bladder and can take air at the surface, sometimes swimming for 10 to 15 yards with its head and

upper half of its body completely out of the water, a phenomenon that is unexplained according to Minnesota game warden Frank Bowstring, since it only takes a moment to get a breath of air. A black Woolly Bugger soaked in your favorite liquid attractant and fished slowly on the bottom near or in weeds is your best bet to nail one of these powerful fish. Oh, don't make the mistake of netting a bowfin: they thrash and spin wildly in a net, often becoming badly entangled and perhaps injuring themselves. I learned this lesson in the Everglades as a boy and haven't forgotten it.

From rocky secondary points, channel drop-offs, steep banks, lily pads, and detached swimming

Above: A secondary point with lily and bulrush growth.

Left: Marty Cecil with a handsome Elktrout cutthroat.

31

floats to milfoil beds, pondweed patches, now-submerged roadbeds and building foundations, bulrushes, and myriad other forms, structure in freshwater is as diverse as it gets. Because of this diversity, the flyfisher must pay close attention to changing conditions of light, temperature, and wind, as well as changes in the structure itself, the habits of the gamefish being targeted, and what is happening under, on, and above the surface of the water.

THE EFFECTS OF THE SUN

The degree of sunlight on structure can play an important role, a fact many flyfishers fail to understand. This point was driven home on Birch Lake in northern Minnesota recently while I threw flies at fat and feisty bluegills and pumpkinseeds. My 5-weight was getting a workout placing small chartreuse poppers within a few feet of the bank amid lily pads, logs, and docks in the late morning and early afternoon, producing a great many fish in about two hours. I took a break for a late lunch and then hit the same water again about four o'clock, but something had changed in the interim: the fish had stopped hitting near the shore.

I backed the boat off and began casting to lily pads mixed with pondweed ("cabbage") and a dock between 10 and 15 feet from the bank and the action instantly picked up again. What had happened?

The direct sunlight striking the water close to the bank earlier in the day had changed. Now the sun was hitting the water at a lower angle and the fish had moved out from the bank to hide in the shadows of the lily pads and cabbage several feet farther out from the bank. There wasn't a single bream anywhere near the bank now, but hordes of them were in the deeper water with spotty shade. The later it got, the farther the fish moved from the bank.

Clouds also affect sunlight's penetration into water, and they can radically change the behavior and feeding impulses of various freshwater gamefish. Some years ago, while casting flies on Minnesota's Portage Lake for bass with guides Steve Tooker and Al Maas, we were having limited results (read: two bass in two hours) under a bright blue sky. Al remarked that things might change when the cirrostratus clouds just off to the northwest got over us, and sure enough, things did change. Immediately the bass turned on and we caught and released 10 in less than an hour; quite an improvement in a short period of time.

The effects of sun on gamefish is the source of much speculation. However, we can surmise that since fish are cold blooded and since many are predators, they move from sun to shade or vice versa to help fine-tune their metabolism and body temperature, and that they use shadows to both hide from predators and attack prey. This latter point was made very clear while I caught those bream. When the sun was at certain angles that allowed me to see well into the water, I

The area in question.

A partially submerged log with lily pads; a classic recipe for bass and bream.

repeatedly saw the big bream scoot out from the shade of some structure (where it had remained unseen by me until it moved) to strike from behind the popper. The fish were obviously using the shade to hide from the pike and largemouth bass and as an

Al Maas holds some of the evidence.

33

Above: A Harris Solitude II with a selection of good panfish flies for probing surface structure.

Right: Juvenile bass learn how to hunt early in life and often hide in dense surface structure.

ambush point to feed on insects that were falling into the water. As far as temperature is concerned, the shallower water close to the bank was a bit warmer in the late morning and early afternoon with direct sunlight hitting it, but it cooled a couple of degrees as the sun began to sink. Now the warmer water was a little farther out and the fish moved to it.

The wind and sun together can produce change in a fish's way of thinking. On Birch Lake, where I was catching the pumpkinseeds and bluegills, there is a large cabbage, coontail, bulrush, and lily bed in a long cove, with the cabbage and coontail being farther out and the bulrushes and lily pads along the bank. On days with a mix of bright sun and some clouds at midday with a nonexistent or light wind, the pike are more likely to be found about 100 yards from shore in 10 to 12 feet of water in the cabbage and milfoil. But on days with wind gusting to 20 knots and similar light conditions, the pike move right up to within a few yards of the bulrushes near the shore in less than 7 feet of water. In both cases they feed actively.

LILY PADS

Lily pads offer the flyfisher a wonderful array of opportunities for several species of gamefish, most notably largemouth bass and panfish such as bluegills and pumpkinseeds. But there is much more to catching fish in lily pads than meets the eye, much more than casting a weedless deer-hair bug into a gap in the pads and hoping a bass eats it.

For our purposes the following information incorporates aquatic plants with broad leaves that rest directly on the surface, such as the yellow waterlily, yellow pondlily, American lotus, watershield, and so on.

Lily Pad Bed Layout

Before you make your first exploratory cast into the pads, study the bed carefully just as a wise trout fanatic studies the water of a stream before making that first cast. You are looking and listening for the same things the trout angler is: feeding and holding fish and places that are likely to hold fish. You are also looking into the water and onto the surface for prey species such as golden shiners, minnows, spiders, and various insects. Oftentimes you will find that determining what the fish are eating is fairly easy, although from time to time this task proves quite challenging. Then again, sometimes what the fish are eating is ridiculously obvious.

Smallish pads.

35

The latter was the case on Birch Lake in the early evening in the second week of July 1997. As soon as the sun dipped below the ridge to the west, a marvelous hatch of white caddisflies took place. The little sedges were fluttering all over the glassy water and the bream went nuts.

Of course, when I first saw the hatch and the fish start to feed, I assumed that because bluegills and pumpkinseeds were so uncouth and gullible they would take nearly any fly I showed them, but I was quite mistaken. The chartreuse popper went entirely ignored, as did the green rubber spider. I switched to a white popper and was quickly rewarded with several nice fish, and a white Muddler received like attention. Sometimes even heathen fish like panfish can be fussy and demand a reasonable imitation as well as some respect.

A patch of lily pads is very much like a community broken up into different neighborhoods, and by studying the entire community you can begin to make reasonable guesses as to where the best action will be found.

The most obvious hot spot to many flyfishers is that gaping hole in the pads, which is popular only because it really is hot so often. But why is it hot? Why would gamefish gather near that opening? The answer is forage activity thereabouts. That small opening affords opportunities for minnows to gather, common water striders (*Gerris remigris*) to skate, whirligigs (*Dineutus*) to cavort, damselflies (*Zygoptera*) and dragonflies (*Anisoptera*) to lay their eggs, and aquatic insects such as mayflies (*Ephemeroptera*) and caddisflies (*Trichoptera*) to hatch into flying adults. With all this prey activity, naturally the opening becomes a prime hunting ground for bass, pickerel, and panfish.

Bed edges and holes, when added to a dock and emergent vegetation like cattails, means fish and often plenty of them.

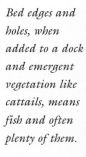

36

That opening has to be fished correctly, however, if you want premium results. Can you determine whether a certain prey species is being taken more than others? If you can, then you must match the hatch or whatever it is feeding upon heavily. If the gamefish are simply eating whatever is available, which is often the case, then you must select a fly that appears both natural and vulnerable to attack and then place that fly in the opening in a way that looks natural.

For instance, if the northern leopard frogs (*Rana pipiens*) are "running" in the late summer and early fall in the upper Midwest, a deer-hair frog would be in order, but frogs don't fall out of the sky, meaning that the fly shouldn't land in the middle of the opening. Instead, it should enter the opening from the top of the surrounding lily pads. And instead of stopping the fly in the middle to give your quarry a "better chance" to catch it—a ridiculous notion when you think about it—scoot the fly right across the opening and don't pause your retrieve until the face of the fly strikes the edge of a pad. Now pause for a moment and wiggle your rod tip back and forth so that the fly wiggles against the edge of the pad, making it appear as though the frog is attempting to get up onto the pad. This retrieve can draw wicked strikes from excited bass and other gamefish.

Another option is to work the edge of the opening with a weedless frog imitation that can only be seen in glimpses as it skirts the edge. When the fish hits, wait until you feel pressure before setting the hook. An immediate set will fre-

The neighborhoods in this lily bed include various densities of the pads, a dock, an overhanging tree, and bulrushes.

37

Come evening, thick pads with a few openings are must fishing.

quently pull the fly from the fish's mouth before the fish has a chance to get it into its mouth. Pressure tells you when to set the hook.

I learned a neat trick from a bass pro in North Carolina that can be adapted to the fly rod. He would use a bullet-shaped light plastic float called the Carolina Floater (which he invented and which is marketed by Betts Tackle) to retrieve a soft plastic curltail grub over thick weeds to a hole in those weeds. When the grub and floater arrived in the opening he would give the rig slack and let the grub sink below the floater right down into the hole. He would then twitch or jig the grub, and often a bass would inhale it a couple of feet down.

To do this with a fly is simple. Use a weighted, weedless Woolly Bugger, Bunny Leech, or similar offering. Retrieve the fly over the top of the weeds until it is over the opening. Now flip some slack line toward it to get it to sink. Twitch and jig the fly several times at various depths until a strike is detected. You know the rest.

A few pads off on their own away from the main bed often hold fish that far too often go unmolested. This is especially true of bluegills, longear sunfish, redear sunfish, redbreast sunfish, and pumpkinseeds. For some reason these species will often take up position hereabouts several feet or even yards from the main bed. Perhaps the competition is a little lighter there.

The edges of beds are also likely locales, and you might be required to keep your fly close to the edge to get consistent attention. Experiment and pay attention.

Many flyfishers fail to realize that lily pads with fully developed pads grow underwater as well as on the surface. This subsurface structure often goes unno-

These few pads
may hold fish
seeking less com-
petition.

ticed, and with it go unnoticed fish. The flyfisher should be continually checking
the pad structure below as well as that on the surface. A sink-tip line can come in
handy when gamefish are feeding contentedly below the surface in these submerged pads and see no reason to come to the surface to eat a fly.

Dense lily pad beds can be intimidating to the uninitiated who fear many
missed strikes and many lost flies in the conundrum of aquatic flora. This is really
where listening can pay off. Panfish take flies in thick pads with a smacking or
kissing sound. When you hear this you know that insect activity within the bed is
encouraging the bream to search the surface for small but plentiful prey, which
they take by sneaking up behind the doomed bug and sucking it in much like a
bass sucks in a crawdad or plastic worm. A small weedless popper placed right in
the thick of things and gently twitched and wiggled can be highly productive.
Obviously the fish is oftentimes going to become fouled in the lily stalks, but
constant, steady pressure will often free the fish from the stalks.

Brush underneath pads is perfect structure for bass and bream, and strips of
pads in open water can attract and hold a surprisingly large population of fish.

A final tip on lily pads. When all else fails, try a small, shiny black popper
between 1/4 and 1/2 inch long with dark rubber legs between 1/8 and 1/4
inch. This popper can imitate waterlily leaf beetles (*Donacia*), females of which
bore holes through pads to lay their eggs on the underside. Minnows and predatory aquatic insects feed on the larvae (mostly before the larvae spin shelters).
This activity draws panfish and bass.

A good-sized popper chugged hard over submerged lily pads can wake up a snoozing bass.

Brush added to pads increases its value as structure.

RUSHES AND BULRUSHES

These two plant families are represented by two primary species, with the soft rush (*Juncus effusus*) representing the former and the great bulrush (*Scirpus validus*) representing the latter. They aren't to be confused with the much more diminutive spikerush (*Eleocharis engelmanni*), which seldom offers any substantial structure.

Rushes and bulrushes offer a very different form of structure. Lacking broad leaves that lie on the surface and therefore unable to provide excellent cover and concealment, these plants attract not so much largemouth and typical bream like bluegill and pumpkinseeds but rather rock bass and smallmouth bass. They grow from bottoms more made of hardpan, gravel, and small rocks than softer bottoms that lily pads prefer, and this is why rock bass and smallmouth are much more likely to be encountered here.

These plants can be just as maddening to the newcomer as lily pads. Long casts made into them tend to wrap around the tough stalks and flies are routinely hung up. (The great bulrush can grow to 10 feet, the soft rush to 6 feet.) Instead of making those long casts, shorten them up while working the rushes quietly. Short, straight casts that don't flair to one side at the end of the cast are what's called for. On the up side, fish hooked in rushes tend not to be as troublesome as those hooked in dense lily pads.

I have found that in many cases the fish might be anywhere in the rushes. Thorough coverage of the structure is important, therefore, so ensure that your fly hits the water every couple of feet.

One of the most amusing and audacious little fish in rushes is the rock bass. This tough guy hits hard and puts on a good show for the entire fight. The heaviest rod used should be no more than a 5-weight, with a 3- or 4-weight being even better. Typical panfish poppers in yellow, white, green, and chartreuse are what is needed. Work the rushes in their entirety and don't be expecting the numbers of fish found when going after bluegills and related sunfish, since rock bass are a bit more territorial and like some elbow (fin?) room.

This strip of pads in open water provides refuge where none other can be found.

PONDWEED

Pondweed is perhaps the most important single family of aquatic flora in North American eutrophic (warm, shallow lakes that are rich in nutrients) and mesotrophic (less fertile) lakes. Muskellunge, northern pike, chain pickerel, large-mouth bass, bowfin, bullheads, an array of panfish, and dozens of species of bait-fish and insects depend on pondweed. Naturally, this means that the flyfisher must become master of the pondweed.

Bulrushes.

Flyfishing pondweed calls for clear and directed strategy. Flyfishers who approach pondweed with a haphazard "just start casting" attitude may catch fish, but they will not be as consistently successful as the flyfisher who studies the conditions and focuses on the most likely areas and depths of the pondweed. Pondweed grows to heights of about 8 feet and comes in single plants, small groups of plants, and beds that may be hundreds of yards long and wide. It might be thick with only inches between plants, and it might be fairly open with yards between plants. It can grow on its own or be found associated with waterlillies, bulrushes, tapegrass, eelgrass, arrowhead, and water plantain, among other plants.

Streamers and leech patterns are two of the most effective patterns when

42

Far left: Pondweed.

Left: A classic Wollaston Lake northern pike. (Photo courtesy of Scott Anderson and Wollaston Lake Lodge.)

fishing pondweed. Floating and sink-tip lines are all that's required, and it is important to cover the entire water column, because bass, northerns, and muskellunge will all hide deep in the stuff when they feel it necessary, such as during midday or when boaters are putting them down by creating a racket up top.

FALLEN TREES

Fallen trees represent some of the best, most focused structure available, focused meaning that the fish are likely to be concentrated in a comparatively tight area. Largemouth bass are perhaps the most sought-after species when it

43

The author with a northern pike taken in Minnesota's Leech Lake on a large pondweed bed. (Mike Roiger photo.)

comes to gamefish holding on a fallen tree, but other gamefish orient on trees, too, with crappie and other panfish being near the top of the list.

Most flyfishers who don't understand how to work a fallen tree make the mistake of not covering the tree in its entirety. They don't understand that

— more than one fish might be on that tree;
— the tree is likely to have locations along it that are more attractive than others; and that
— there are likely to be areas along the tree that are difficult—but not impossible—to access that are holding the biggest fish, such as the underside of the tree where there may be a depression in the bottom.

The first step in working a fallen tree is to not begin casting at it as soon as you arrive but to examine it closely. What you are looking for are specific locations along the tree that appear to be good lies. Bass like the underside of limbs and dead space between the limbs, as well as beneath the trunk. Panfish prefer bushy limbs.

Once you have selected some prime spots to try, consider where you can best position yourself so as to not spook other fish that may be nearby holding in other locations on the tree. This is quite important. Far too many flyfishers give no thought at all to this concern, and they end up spooking all the other fish thereabouts, and they often have no idea they have done so. The spot from which you cast must allow you to properly present the fly to the fish and also allow you to get

Where do you start?

Depressions beneath the limbs on the tree's underside often hold the largest fish.

45

the fish out from the tree with minimal sound and activity. So we see that the other fish may be afraid of your shadow or outline (or that of your boat) and the sound (vibrations) and sight of another fish in a struggle with some unseen opponent—you.

It is best to work from the outside in so that you are not forced to bring a fighting fish out from the inner reaches of the tree past other fish on the outer reaches. Fish will usually flee from other fish in an obvious struggle. This is the same principle as shooting grouse from a single tree. As a boy, when I found several grouse in a single tree, I would shoot the one on the lowest branch first, then work my way up. Oftentimes, the ones above would not fly. But if I selected the uppermost bird first, that bird's falling past the others would spook them. (Yes, this was before I was informed that such hunting practices as shooting birds in trees was, although legal, somewhat less than sporting. It was also a time when members of a less-than-wealthy family of seven—not including a Labrador, up to 12 beagles, a cat, chickens, and several rabbits—in rural Maine needed every bit of dinner they could get.)

FLOODED TIMBER

Flooded timber is one of those types of structure that gets the flyfisher's heart thumping, because it just looks fishy. My first experience with heavy, standing flooded timber was on San Diego's Otay Lake with Jeff Carothers. We were after bass and found them among the trees of the big impoundment known for big bass. In fact, Otay is considered by many to be one of the leading lakes suspected of having the potential for giving up a world-record largemouth.

What you can't see beneath the water is always as important as what you can see above the water.

Recently I was casting flies with the editor of *Fly Fish America*, Bill Battles, on a small pond in Colorado that has some standing timber on the east and south side. Bill had just come into a nice Hexagraph rod and decided to see what was hanging out in the trees. It didn't surprise me when he returned a while later with a report telling of three nice bass found in the woods. It seems that timber, regardless of what water it is found in, holds fish, most often bass.

But a word to the wise first: your leader and tippet will be taking more abuse in standing timber than many other forms of structure. Upgrade accordingly.

Like working a single fallen tree, flooded timber requires certain tactics. The layout of that timber is the governing factor in deciding how to work the timber, and working it can be very much like deciphering a lily bed.

Flooded timber might just as easily be younger trees rather than genuine timber.

Straight Edges

In timber where a group of trees presents a linear or straight edge, flies presented in variations along the linear edge will receive more attention than those presented along unremarkable stretches. Indentations, curves, points, and other anomalies attract more bass. It really is that simple.

Patches

On waters with an assortment of timber, seek out the patches that stand off on their own, even if those patches consist of only a few trees. These sequestered stands often produce more bass per square yard than any other form of timber structure because they focus the bass in a confined area, making flies substantially more vulnerable to attack.

Shade

One of the reasons bass (and other gamefish as well) like flooded timber is because it affords them comfort and ambush sites in the way of shade. Bass are ambushers by nature; therefore they are constantly on the lookout for a place from

Shade is a critical reason why gamefish find flooded timber so enticing. Note the ring rise.

which to safely launch an attack on some unsuspecting prey species and do so from a comfortable location out of the annoying rays of the sun. It follows, therefore, that flies presented in shady areas will draw more strikes than those presented in sunny areas. And the longer the fly remains in the shade, the more likely a bass will strike it. By stripping the fly along the length of a shadow created by a tree, as opposed to across the shadow, you increase the chances of a strike.

The past-and-pause retrieve plays upon the bass' instinctive strike reaction to a change in prey's actions. It is best performed with a typically saltwater-oriented retrieve that allows the flyfisher to strip in the fly without having to pause between strips. Capt. Bill Harris, an Atlantic Beach, North Carolina, guide has demonstrated this retrieve's effectiveness for me many times while striper fishing on the once prolific Neuse River (now in dire straits due to agricultural runoff and heinous commercial overfishing by what many feel is one of the most destructive commercial fishing fleets in the nation), but it is equally effective on largemouth in flooded timber.

Cast a popper, deer-hair bug, or other surface fly past the tree several feet. Place the rod under one arm and retrieve the line with both hands revolving around in each other so that the retrieve is continuous (a stripping basket is nice; author, flyfishing instructor, and fly designer Lou Tabory has probably done more to promote the use of a stripping basket than any other flyfisher). When the fly is immediately adjacent to the tree, stop the retrieve and get the rod back in your hands. Do not move the fly for several seconds. If nothing happens, wiggle the rod tip a bit to make the fly wiggle slightly. If nothing happens, continue the retrieve as before.

The twitch-and-pause is good medicine for bass and bream hanging in brush amid standing timber. The fly is presented right in the brush and is twitched and paused repeatedly until a strike comes. This is especially effective during periods of cold when gamefish are less active.

If the bass are holding a few feet below the surface and visibility is poor and the water cold, which make bass lethargic and less than willing to come to the surface for a fly, switch to a sink-tip line and short leader (4 feet or so) and tie on something like a Dahlberg Diver. If the water is deep enough, the sink-tip will

The correct retrieve between these two snags will force an otherwise recalcitrant fish to strike.

drag the fly under water. A strip-strip-strip-pause retrieve will work the fly in an enticing, undulating action and the pause will make the fly begin to rise back toward the surface. This action is often hard for a bass to turn down. (This is an old red drum trick used by guides like Capt. Bramblett Bradham.)

STUMPS

The Dover Reservoir in the New Hampshire town of the same name is a warren of stumps that many fat largemouths call home. The reservoir is filled with lots of baitfish and many frogs, and it is especially worthwhile to fish this little water at night when the wind has lain down. The sounds coming from the stumps tell the tale of many hapless creatures being eaten by the aggressive bass, and if there ever was a situation when a fly would prove hard if not impossible to beat, this is it. Deceivers, deer-hair bugs, Mouserats, pencil poppers, and Bunny Leeches (the latter worked vigorously right below the surface) all do well.

In the daytime the bass are less aggressive, although they still feed heavily. Their tactics change with the light, however, with the bass feeding more heavily below the surface, quite opposite to what goes on at night. The reason for this change is the bass' good vision at night as contrasted to its quarry's less than good vision. This makes baitfish and frogs more vulnerable when they are swimming around on the surface, which they try to avoid during the day, and silhouetted in openings against the moonlight. (When is the last time you saw frogs

Weedless deer-hair bugs are an excellent choice when fishing thick growth in the stump fields.

Soft-bodied poppers like these Mr. Bob's cause bass to hold on longer after the initial strike. No, I am not the Mr. Bob who makes these; I don't know who he is. I do know that his flies work, however.

50

Fish holding on winter stumps can be tough nuts to crack.

swimming in the open during broad daylight? They know better.) Come sunup, the baitfish and frogs retire to structure like the stumps, especially when those stumps have some weed growth around them. The bass know this and slowly prowl the stumps or select one stump and hang tightly on it to wait for an unsuspecting baitfish. Prowling bass also get far back into the stumps in the heaviest weed growth where they can sneak up on frogs.

Weedless flies, therefore, are what's called for when back in the thickest stump fields with the thickest weed growth. Those flies should also be large, with something akin to a gaudy Dahlberg Diver in green and brown being a top choice for a frog imitation. High-energy retrieves that force the fly to be noisy are needed.

On the outer edges of the stump field, try a weighted Bunny Leech worked slowly and deliberately right next to and around every stump you see. Such an obviously defenseless victim like this can be very hard for a bass to turn down, especially when it is worked all around his structure and right under his nose.

WATER HYACINTH

Imported from the New World tropics decades ago and released in southern Florida, the water hyacinth is now considered the most noxious aquatic weed in the world. It multiplies at a rate seldom seen elsewhere in the plant kingdom, increasing its number by one thousand times in only 2 months. And although water hyacinth is a tropical plant, it has now spread into other parts of the South. It can literally choke a waterway to the point where only an airboat can pass through it, and it drifts with the wind and current. Control measures are extensive, but only one animal species eats water hyacinth, and that is the endangered manatee (or sea cow).

The only saving grace of water hyacinth is the structure it provides for so many living things, from the tiniest microscopic life to giant Florida-strain largemouth bass and the impressively armed alligator gar.

Having spent some of my childhood in central and south Florida, I learned early the subtleties of water hyacinth and how fish relate to it. At great risk to life and limb—every small boy in Florida knows that 'gators and water moccasins lurk under every patch of water hyacinth just waiting for a misplaced hand to make an ill-advised appearance—I would frequently lift up some water hyacinth to examine the things making their home in the roots. I was never disappointed, for the root masses were infested with a plethora of aquatic life, which I knew were fed upon by minnows, which in turn were eaten by bream and baby bass, themselves being swallowed by big bass, mudfish, and toothy gar.

Small mats of water hyacinth occasionally hold big largemouths, but more often than not it will be a smaller bass that is found beneath the weeds. When mats are pushed up against roots and other more firm structure, the chances of finding a large bass there substantially increase. A large, weighted Bunny Leech can bring about a struggle between you and a potentially double-digit largemouth, provided you work in close to the primary structure that is probably mostly hidden by the water hyacinth. Worked down between individual weeds and into small openings between weeds and then jigged and twitched, this fly and tactic can be most productive. Make sure you cover every bit of primary structure below the water hyacinth, which can be tricky because of the structure's being hidden.

But largemouths prefer the golden shiner to all else, and the bigger the shiner the better. Largemouths think nothing of inhaling a golden shiner that weighs nearly a pound, which means that large flies will often be required. Saltwater flies designed for stripers and other hefty gamefish can be brought into play here, as can an old snook trick: along a water hyacinth edge, toss a few small shiners. Largemouths a little way back in the mat will come to investigate. Get your largest shiner imitation in there and begin stripping quickly and erratically.

IT WAS A DARK AND STORMY NIGHT

Darkness is certainly the most underfished time, especially when it comes to flyfishing. This is indeed a shame because many gamefish feed at night, particular-

ly brown trout and largemouth and smallmouth bass. Some of the largest brown trout ever caught have been caught at night in Western reservoirs, and any bass fanatic will tell you that catching bass at night is frequently the most exciting aspect of the sport.

Bass around almost any kind of structure at night are after insects, baitfish (which can't see as well at night as bass can, remember), frogs (which are busy focusing on catching insects and often seem to forget that they, too, are being hunted), and crayfish. Lighted docks are great targets; they attract insects that are fed upon by baitfish, frogs, and bass, producing a triple whammy of sorts: the bass come to eat the frogs and baitfish, which have come to eat the insects, which are also fed upon by the bass. Add the swarms of crayfish that parade around the bottom at night and you begin to see why flyfishing at night for bass is a very good idea.

Streamers and large surface flies like poppers and deer-hair bugs are choice. A large Gray Ghost or green-over-white Deceiver will frequently bring truly vicious attacks from prowling bass, and poppers and deer-hair bugs are inhaled with an attitude.

Chapter 4

Saltwater

Bottom

Structure

Captain Rodney Smith works a fly along the bottom of the Banana River Lagoon.

M any miles off the coast of North Carolina, the venerable *Nancy Lee III*, a classic 42-foot sportfisher built by her captain, Lee Manning, rode the gentle swells over an unseen bottom. Lee, one of the most experienced charter captains on the North Carolina coast with three decades of professional sport fishing under his belt, cut the engines back as we approached the bottom structure we were looking for, far more than 100 feet below.

Flyfishing bottom structure that is well in excess of 100 feet down? Yes. And, well, no.

I was about to get a lesson from the master captain on how bottom structure, even when it is hundreds of feet below your hull, relates directly to what is happening on the surface.

It was an unusually calm summer day approximately 38 miles out of Bogue Inlet, that roily, never-to-be-trusted doorway to Onslow Bay and beyond just north of the little village of Swansboro on the Bogue Banks. We had steamed at full throttle since making our way out of the inlet and the sun was just gaining a foothold on the horizon when we arrived over the structure that Lee suspected would hold gamefish from top to bottom. It wasn't long until Lee was once again proved right.

55

The author with a yellowfin tuna taken many miles off Cabo San Lucas. Bottom structure attracted this fish, which was caught on top. (Fran Milner photo.)

We—Lee, mate Jeff Warren, and I—saw them coming at the same time: false albacore, those powerful, lovely members of the tuna family that appear and disappear often with little warning. Although they weren't feeding especially heavily, the baitfish they were chasing being loosely schooled up at the time, I knew that a gray-and-white Deceiver would get their attention, provided I could get the fly in front of them before the fish sped past on their way south. Lee pushed the throttle down and spun the boat to starboard, which allowed me a quick double haul to get the fly where it needed to be. The first chunky fish to see the fly gulped it and departed for Savannah, my 9-weight rod bending to the cork and line fleeing my reel in a blur.

Fifteen minutes later, the powerful tuna was brought aboard, my arms aching. As I admired the colorful fish, I couldn't help but marvel at the fact that we were far from the sight of land and in hundreds of feet of water, but gamefish were nevertheless relating to the structure of the bottom many fathoms below. I was reminded that bottom structure, to some degree, governs the actions of more gamefish than most people realize, even when that bottom is nowhere to be seen. A few moments later, a king mackerel intercepted the same Deceiver, reiterating that diversity and fast action are the name of the game when flyfishing over deep-water structure in the ocean.

THE DOMINO EFFECT

Bottom structure in salt water affects most gamefish, regardless of whether they

are considered primarily surface or near-surface feeders, such as dolphin, wahoo, and false albacore. This is so because the bottom structure has a kind of domino or ripple effect on all gamefish passing over it. It begins with the structure itself.

That day off the North Carolina coast the bottom structure was a stretch of rough bottom set amid an otherwise unremarkable, featureless bottom. Those jumbled rocks are home to an assortment of marine life that clings to the rocks, which attract small baitfish like cigar minnows, which in turn are fed upon by spottail pinfish, vermilion snapper, gray triggerfish, and other bottom dwellers, which attract black grouper, cobia, and great barracuda. All this activity does not go unnoticed from above, where king and Spanish mackerel, dolphin, yellowfin tuna, false albacore, wahoo, and a slough of other killers prowl.

But how does one recognize productive bottom structure when that structure is deep in the brine?

Water temperature variations and upwellings are the answer to this riddle. Ocean currents come in many strengths, widths, and depths. Currents that move along the bottom, which are very common and can't always be detected on the surface, strike structure and well up toward the surface, bringing colder water upward and moving baitfish along this kind of escalator as well. Nutrients are also moved upward, bringing even more life toward the sun. As the nutrients and baitfish are swept upward, gamefish patrolling the area take note and converge on the bounty from the deep.

A yellowfin tuna captured off the North Carolina coast.

This is how gamefish like dolphin, yellowfin, and wahoo are all connected to the bottom, even though they are primarily found close to the surface. The flyfisher who locates bottom structure that forces deep-water currents upward can take great advantage of it by positioning himself at or near the upwelling's apogee.

But not all bottom structure has the ability to redirect a bottom current. Sunken vessels, insignificant rocks, small ledges, and the like in deep water don't have the ability to deflect the current high enough to be of any use, and slow bottom currents don't generate enough speed to be deflected. Large ridges, humps, and ledges, on the other hand, do have what it takes to redirect a bottom current, and if that current is strong, all the better.

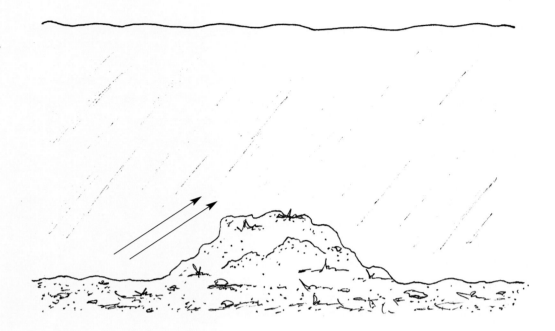

A deep-water current and how it is deflected toward the surface.

Exploitation

To fully exploit an upwelling, the flyfisher must have a few things in his bag of tricks, including a Loran C or Global Positioning System (GPS) unit, a depth finder, and a lot of chum.

The Loran C system of navigation is still up and running as of this writing, but there are tentative plans for it to be replaced by GPS. The Loran towers require maintenance and they frequently go down, and many believe the system has run its course. However, over the years probably every major and minor piece of structure on the ocean floor off North America has been plotted using Loran C, and anglers have the coordinates plugged into their systems. GPS coordinates are not anywhere near being fully compiled yet, meaning that if the Loran C is taken off line, many specific fishing locations will be lost. So it looks like we will be using the Loran C until the GPS coordinates are completely logged in.

GPS gives excellent accuracy, and with sonar you can plot fish hanging on the structure. You really do need both if you want to fully exploit an upwelling in deep water many miles offshore.

And finally there is the chum. A chum line run so that the slick drifts back over the upwelling is what you want, and that slick must be carefully controlled. You want it to be mostly made up of tiny pieces of bait, not many large chunks at all, since you are trying to entice baitfish into the slick first, which will be followed by hungry and aggressive gamefish. Too many large chunks of bait in the slick will end up feeding the gamefish, and that is what you don't want. You want them interested, not well fed. Every now and then, just to get them fired up, you can toss in a few juicy chunks and a few livies, but that's it. Teasers (a live baitfish tied to a heavy leader with no hook) and a Judas stick will add to the melee and make the fun all the more exciting for all parties, including the fish.

One person should always be ready with a fly as another chums and works the teaser. Be watchful for approaching gamefish. As the one you want comes barreling in toward the teaser, the teaser is picked up and replaced by the fly. This is an excellent tactic for amberjack, barracuda, king and Spanish mackerel, bonito, false albacore, and many other saltwater gamefish.

INSHORE REEFS, ROCKS, AND LEDGES

Perhaps the most overlooked saltwater flyfishing opportunities are those offered by inshore reefs, rocks, and ledges, although such structure, in the past 10 years or so, has received an ever-increasing amount of attention. Still, most of this structure goes untried year after year. The reason for this is because so few flyfishers take the time to explore and study this structure, even though there are dozens of species of quite worthy gamefish living there, ranging from stripers, spadefish (a most excellent quarry that appears to be a giant angelfish), grouper, snapper, and barracuda, to name a few.

Flyfishing on shallow reefs, rocks, and ledges can be as simple as drifting or anchoring over the structure and working a sinking line to maneuvering in close to awash ledges and getting in a cast or two before you must quickly back the boat out to prevent becoming structure yourself. Chum lines can work here as well under some circumstances, but not always.

Sometimes, as is the case with working the surface above offshore bottom structure, it is going to be tricky getting your fly to the larger fish. Barracuda, amberjack, and snapper are notorious for this, with the smaller fish occupying the top of the water column and the larger fish hanging below them. The situation can be quite infuriating. One of the best ways around this is to make your cast long with a super-fast-sinking line such as a Teeny or Orvis Depth Charge well beyond the action near the boat. Allow the line to sink deep and then begin your retrieve. This can bring your fly into the larger fish at their level before the little guys ever have a chance to see it.

Especially in the case of awash rocks and ledges, the current can play a critical role in where the gamefish are. This is often precisely the situation off the coast of New England with stripers that are in tight against the structure and that structure is active, meaning that the current, waves, and wind are all doing their thing to make the approach a bit dicey. Two people in the boat are almost mandatory here; one driving and one casting. You must get in, get within range, make the cast and retrieve, and get out, then approach again. To plan the best

*Great
barracuda.
(George
Poveromo
photo.)*

approach, it helps to study the structure and the effects of the wind, waves, and current first.

Inshore reefs, rocks, and ledges are natural fish attractors that are greatly affected by tide, current, and forage availability. Such structure may be a hot prospect on the ebbing tide, but when the tide is flooding the structure might be vacant. Experimentation and attention to detail go a long way toward learning the tricks of the tide.

The same applies to currents, which move laterally but can also move vertically when structure alters their course. Currents, however, are not to be confused with the tide, which only moves vertically. Inshore currents are primarily products of the tide, but the sun, wind, and structure can also affect them. Gamefish know that the tide will carry food from the hinterlands to them as they wait near the mouth of the river or stream, and they will use ambush points adjacent to structure that is being swept over or past by current. The forage fish moving with the current know this and routinely move along quickly in an attempt to evade attack by the predators they know are waiting thereabouts. Fast retrieves that mimic scared baitfish bring more strikes than casual retrieves imitating a baitfish that doesn't seem to be bothered by the fact that killers are nearby, preying on the gamefish's instinctive reaction to attack something that appears to be trying to escape. Oftentimes you do not need a particularly precise imitation of the baitfish.

One situation that is almost never exploited by flyfishers is Atlantic spadefish holding over inshore reefs, rocks, and wrecks in warm water. A powerful member of the butterflyfishes (*Ephippidae*) that can grow to 3 feet in length and weigh 14 pounds, this excellent gamefish often focuses on one thing to eat to the exclusion of all else: blueball jellyfish. But when blueballs aren't available, spadefish eat all manner of marine invertebrates, so a shrimp pattern can be effective. Sight-casting to spades can be thrilling when the wind lies down over an inshore reef, the water is clear, and the current slacks off. A sinking line is usually needed to get your fly down to the spadefish, but sometimes they are willing to leave the safety of their structure and come toward the surface for a meal that appears promising.

Permit are another species frequently found over wrecks, reefs, and coral heads, although most flyfishers incorrectly assume that these highly prized and remarkably strong gamefish are more often found on the subtropical and tropical flats of the Florida Keys and Caribbean. The truth is that permit spend most of their lives in deeper water and only move to the flats when they want a change of scenery and some different forage. Permit are naturally curious fish that may come up off the wreck (or other bottom structure) and approach your boat, making them vulnerable to a fly, but many flyfishers chum them up, too.

It is important to use the proper fly tackle when fishing for permit over bottom structure. Unlike an empty South Andros or Exuma flat, wrecks and reefs give the permit an opportunity to sound and cut your leader on something sharp. This means that a heavier, stiffer rod and tough line and leader are in order over a wreck so that you can put the pressure to the permit and turn it before it has a chance to cut you off. So, that 8- or 9-weight rod you use for permit on the flats must be upgraded to a bare minimum of a 10-weight, preferably an 11- or 12-weight. Certain cays off Belize offer some of the best opportunities to cast flies at big permit hanging on reefs and wrecks.

Don't think for a moment that permit only accept crab imitations. They regularly take baitfish and shrimp imitations as well.

The many wrecks and rocks lying in Southern California waters often hold excellent numbers of calico bass, but these tough cookies won't be coming up to take a peek at your boat. If you want these bass on the fly, chum and live anchovies are the way to go. Once they have been enticed up, a sink-tip line in the 8- to 10-weight category is what you'll need to get a hold of them and keep them from breaking off in the kelp. Be on the lookout for barracuda and white seabass while you are out there. Dark green-over-white Deceivers, Sar-Mul-Macs, and Bob Popovics' 3-D Baitfish are top flies.

Chumming over bottom structure is a game of current speed. The most common mistake flyfishers make is to anchor too closely to the structure, which causes the chum to drift over it before the chum has a chance to sink down to the level of the fish. Practice and pay attention. If nothing comes in to the chum line within a few minutes, reposition and begin again.

FLATS

When most anglers think of flats, they picture the Florida Keys and a flats boat floating on crystal-clear water with a flyfisher casting to a giant tarpon. And that scene is played out almost every day in the Keys, but flats can be found from the Northeast to Texas, in Central America, and from Mexico to Alaska. Yes, the flats are everywhere, but finding one is the easy part. Successfully fishing one can be anything but easy.

Flats are places of great contradictions that are governed by weather and water and what's available. One moment a certain flat can appear like something off the cover of *Fly Fishing in Salt Waters*, with every fish in the neighborhood lined up to take your fly, and the next moment it can appear menacing and ugly and evil, a place of dark water and darker clouds scuttling in from the ocean that scatter fish before them like so many Iraqi draftees before the 2nd Marine Division. It ain't pretty, albeit most memorable and oftentimes downright frightening.

You have never felt so naked and helpless as you do when a subtropical thunderstorm bears down on you and your flat from seaward, obviously intent on doing you great harm in a graphic manner. Brevity being valued, I recall the sparse proclamation of one guide with whom I was fishing in Florida who, upon turning around and spying a murderous-looking squall heading our way at a most disturbing rate while I continued casting in utter ignorance of the Grim Reaper's imminent arrival; two words which shall forever remain branded on my gray matter, one of which polite company and an annoyingly efficient and insistent editor refuse to put here:

"Oh, ...!"

Naturally, being a Marine and utterly fearless in the face of everything but an unannounced visit from a process server bearing a summons and announcing a paternity suit, I refused to be intimidated by the presumptuous meteorological manifestation and kept casting, although my guide will swear that I "shrieked like a banshee and tried to get into the live well." Of course, he's a known liar.

Halibut are another gamefish of the flats seldom targeted by the flyfisher. I first went after these strong gamefish on a mud flat between the San Diego bait barge and the submarine pens in San Diego Bay. No, we weren't supposed to be there, and some sailor kept shouting at us from shore that he was going to send for the "shallow-water sailors" (Coast Guard) if we didn't get away from his pre-

The flats take time to learn— a lifetime.

cious submarines, but the halibut were holding in about 8 feet of water and were taking Clousers fished right on the bottom in short strips. We would catch four or five and then get a spotted sand bass, followed by a few more halibut. We fished for about 20 minutes and then got out of there, afraid that the Navy was going to unleash one of its top secret killer porpoises on us, which they keep in pens near the subs.

Flats have to be figured out and then figured out again, for they change not only in appearance but in productivity, with a cold front being the most omnipotent foe of flats fish; covered with shallow water and often only low-growth, sparse vegetation (eelgrass, turtle grass, widgeon grass), water temperature on a flat can plummet rapidly and drive fish off while giving them the most serious form of lockjaw. But when the water warms back up, a benevolent current sweeps across the flat from a channel, and the wind lies down, the flat can be a wondrous place, a place filled with mystery and excitement, challenge and awe, surprise and sweat. It's the details that make the flats so much fun, such as knowing when to switch to a pink Gotcha with no eyes on the flats around Long Cay in Belize, where you may be fishing in 8 inches of water, and when to go with a Deep Shrimp.

There is nothing quite like flyfishing the flats.

I think that, perhaps more than any other factors, stealth, a knowledge of your quarry, and efficient casting are the three most important aspects of flats flyfishing. Bonefish, redfish, snook, permit, spotted seatrout, tarpon, and even heathen fish like barracuda can be and usually are skittish and wary, ready to flee at warp speed if they even think that something is amiss. An angler's silhouette, slapped line, dropped soda can, bumped net handle, even a stubbed toe, can all lead to a vacant flat faster than a Sunday morning televangelist can get into your checking account. Consider yourself warned.

A great many flies will take flats fish, and I seriously doubt that one could be proven to be always better than another, which makes your knowledge of your quarry more important than selecting the proverbial best fly. (The reason why there is no one best fly is because flats predators dine on such a disparate array of forage that there are few situations in which only one fly that imitates one species—even one gender of one species—will work. Granted, there are times when one fly will prove better than all the rest in a very specific instance, such as during a palolo worm hatch, but these cases are the exception and not the rule.) You should become an expert at your quarry's behavior if you intend to master the flats, for you are going to need every shred of knowledge available.

A typical example of this is the tarpon, which, despite its size, can suddenly appear very close to you and be just as easily coming on as swimming away. If your luck dictates that the tarpon is swimming away and you cast your fly beyond the fish and strip back toward it, you stand an excellent chance of frightening the tarpon so badly that it flees in abject terror at the sight of your fly bearing down

64

on it. It isn't the fly per se that the tarpon is afraid of, but rather the fact that the fly is doing something very unnatural—coming at the tarpon—and that means that something is wrong on the flat, and something wrong on the flat is transmitted to the tarpon's brain in a one-word sentence: *Danger!* If you watch a tarpon feed on baitfish, you will notice that the prey scoots ahead of and away from the tarpon at an angle almost all the time. Tarpon are used to this and expect it of their prey. When a mullet suddenly comes racing at the tarpon, the tarpon's instinct tells it that trouble is afin and it is time to go, now. The same can be said for red drum, which, although they feed mostly along the bottom (hence their inferior mouths), will often bolt if they so much as see a rod wave. And bonefish, although bottom feeders also, seem to know where every baby mangrove is within the length of your tippet, leader, line, and backing. They will run straight for that foot-tall mangrove shoot like a politician making for a fund raiser.

The little things you notice and know are what catch more fish on the flats. Lefty Kreh, in his *Advanced Fly Fishing Techniques* (probably the most fact-filled flyfishing book ever written), drives this point home when discussing bonefish. The old master notes that the darker or thicker the "mud" (a cloud of bottom material, often marl, raised by a bonefish or school of bonefish as they feed by blowing a stream of water at the bottom to uncover a morsel of food), the fresher it is, meaning that the bonefish are near, and the larger the mud, the bigger the bonefish, generally speaking. He goes on to say that experienced bonefish hands can "track" a bonefish across the flat this way, and he adds that fresh blowholes are more well defined. Lefty also notes that when bonefish work a flat, they can eat many of the prey species there and will move to a different flat, often nearby, that offers fresh possibilities.

This is the kind of precise information that you need to become the best flats man you can, and we are fortunate to have people like Lefty to tell us of these things so that we can get a bit ahead without having to spend more than four decades on the water. It seems to me that oftentimes the best equipment the fly-fisher can have is a book written by someone who has been there and done that.

Finally, efficient casting is essential. Time and again, a situation will present itself that demands of you only the most perfect cast and which will allow you only one cast before the fish is gone. Watch a guide get a new client in the boat: the first thing he will do when everything is stored and ready to go is ask to see the client's casting technique. If it is falling short in any way, the guide will give a lesson and check for improvement, especially with the all-important double haul and how to release line on the back cast.

It is typical to be on the flats and have a pod of bonefish foraging in front of you in such a way that you must maintain a low profile while getting off an accurate cast that lands a few feet in front of the feeding fish, close enough to be seen when you strip but not so close that you spook the school. Casting mastery is an

A brace of bone-fish tail on a Long Cay flat, Belize.

absolute must, with minimal false casts and the rod canted to one side to reduce the possibility of your casting motion being seen by the fish. Short, quick strips with the fly being moved away from the fish are what generally bring strikes. This is because small crabs and shrimp move in short, quick strips, so to speak. All this involves estimating the speed of the pod and adjusting your cast in midstroke to present the fly in just the right location in just the right way.

Schools of bones moving toward you can be the most difficult to judge. It is better to cast short than long, because the fly moving among the fish as they pass over it or the line landing on or too close to the fish will almost surely spook them.

If you can't cast quickly, far, and accurately, do whatever it takes to acquire that skill before you hit the flats.

Wind on the Flats

Wind is a critical factor in where and how many flats fish feed, particularly bones. The riddle lies in prevailing winds, structure, and how bonefish prefer to feed.

Bonefish are some of the laziest, most casual foragers on the flats, preferring to slowly graze along a flat and rummage for easy-to-catch morsels like shrimp. They therefore prefer the lee side of flats and cays where winds are gentle and the bottom undisturbed, making forage easy to find and catch. When the wind shifts and riles a flat, the bones depart for calmer climes and won't return until things settle down. In the interim they hide out in channels and cuts, which are precisely where prey species go when the wind drives them from the flat, and bonefish will even forage in mangrove roots, provided the tide is high enough. The obvious answer is to station yourself between the mangroves and the nearest cut or channel to intercept the bonefish on the falling tide as they depart for deeper water.

Recently I spent a couple days on the water with Capt. Rodney Smith. Both

66

days were pretty windy but we found ways to get around that. For example, we worked a small, sheltered flat behind a tiny islet on the Banana River Lagoon and found jacks, specks, and ladyfish. And despite the wind, we found large reds and specks on the western shore of the lagoon. We fished only those two spots all day and were rewarded for being patient and thinking like the fish we caught, in that we correctly assumed that the small, protected flat would hold some fish because of the drop-off it had and that the broad, wind-blown flat would hold bigger fish and probably a huge redfish or two because it usually did just that. (The redfish tipped the scales at about 38 pounds.)

Finally, remember not to make the mistake of thinking flats are exclusive to the subtropics, because they certainly are not. The Northeast offers excellent flats fishing, especially Massachusetts and Maine, where stripers, bluefish, and flounder are all readily available. The South is also excellent, with places like Charleston offering plenty of action.

Chapter 5

Freshwater Bottom Structure

You can often judge the slope found under-water by that found above, as here in the Cascades. Sometimes reading and understanding the water is simple and straightforward.

The road pretty much stops at the overgrown apple trees just beyond the abandoned village of Redington, once a stop on the narrow-gauge railway that made its way up from Farmington in years gone by. The two-track is made of dirt and conifer needles, of course, and winds its way along Cold Stream, Redington Stream, and the South Branch of the Dead River in Maine's brooding Redington Pond Range, through a forest of mountain ash, spruce, maple, fir, and birch, until a footpath takes you the remainder of the way to the pond.

The pond draws you to it, but you cannot help pausing in the village to wonder about its few remaining buildings and how they helped form the history in these ancient mountains and the loggers who lived and died here. Cloud shadows, a fresh wind, and the quaking, golden leaves of a poplar stand tell of the autumn to come, and you move down the trail, for some unknown reason trying to be as silent as possible.

You cock your head to the east. Was that the whistle of a distant, diminutive steam engine tugging lumber cars up the valley? No, it was just the wind. It must have been just the wind.

The shine of the pond twinkles through the black alders and greets you with the promise of a mystery revealed, of secret brook trout hiding in the roots of white

69

pine stumps now lying on the pond's bottom. Once this was only a shallow depression with a bit of wet resting in the bottom, but the townsfolk of the tiny mountain village built a log and earthen dam at the eastern end of the depression and created the little pond, forming a new, grand headwater of Orbeton Stream. Beaver quickly arrived to add to the project, and soon Redington Falls Stream, with its stunning hidden waterfall in the highlands to the north, created the new pond. Brook trout from the stream soon invaded the chill, crystalline water.

Decades later, the old dam gave way and some of the pond vanished down Orbeton Stream, but Redington still remains, and it is filled with wonderful brookies lurking among the stumps and roots of pines long dead.

These stumps and roots form a marvelous warren of lairs for the trout, and because so few anglers fish this water, the trout are anxious to eat flies cast to them. (I first came to Redington in autumn of 1987 and have since fished it countless times, having seen only two strangers on the water in the years since.) And although dry flies can bring memorable results when the mayflies and sedges are cavorting on the surface, the largest brookies seem to fall for nymphs fished close to the bottom amid the structure of one-time forest giants.

Redington is best fished from a canoe, as the bottom tends to be a bit soft and the roots and stumps take great amusement in tripping what few anglers venture to her secluded waters. The best trout—plump, lovely jewels of a few pounds—wait amid the stumps for mayfly and caddisfly nymphs and pounce on them with great vigor and strength. There are few gentle takes on Redington.

But the newcomer cannot merely stroll up to this lady and partake of her pleasures. No. Redington keeps her special favors only for those who can interpret what subtle clues she allows and who can understand the complexity of her wiles, for she is an enchantress, a siren adorned with the cloak of an age-old enigma few ever unravel. Shrouded in the mists of time, she waits for her lover.

FORTY ACRES OF BOTTOMLAND

Although 40 acres of bottomland might not prove to be particularly appealing if that acreage were dead center of the Great Dismal Swamp, it would be most attractive if it were forming the bottom of a lake, pond, or reservoir. Indeed, everything is relevant, and before we can hope to fool more fish on the bottom, we must understand the bottom and why it holds fish like a magnet.

Freshwater bottom structure, although very relevant to many potential flyfishing situations, often represents the most intimidating and cryptic of structure to the flyfisher. The reason for this unfortunate situation is that most flyfishers who spend time on the waters in question primarily fish the edges and surface rather than delve into the dark secrets of the bottom. We must change this attitude.

There is a farm pond on the outskirts of Jacksonville, North Carolina, that I fish from time to time. It is a typical farm pond, being small and amusing, but this particular pond holds giant bluegills and bass, and it is the bottom structure that governs the actions of the largest fish in the pond.

In one corner of the pond, unseen and sneaky, lies a tree limb. It rests on the bottom and grants asylum to big, fat "dinner plate" bluegills and belligerent bass, which take great pleasure in wrapping leaders around their wooden walls and roof. John, the owner, has done battle with one colossal largemouth that calls the branch home, but the creature refuses to come to hand and has amassed no minor collection of flies and leaders that now decorate its lair's battlements, much to John's chagrin.

Although this beast occasionally takes smaller flies, it prefers more substantial meals, and it does not come to the surface to feed nearly so often as it does out of sight, down amid the switches and billets of its hideout. This is precisely why we must bring to light the mysteries of freshwater bottom structure, for, like trout in a river, the residents of ponds, lakes, and reservoirs feed much more often under the surface, taking baitfish, crustaceans, and all manner of aquatic insects well out of sight—and therefore out of mind—of prying eyes and inquisitive minds.

RECONNAISSANCE

As you know, I used to collect information—other than that applicable to flyfishing—for a living as a member of more or less good standing in a band of ruffians and errant, globe-trotting thugs and hooligans known as the U.S. Marines. I did this by performing reconnaissance, which is the gathering of raw data for later refinement and dissemination as intelligence. Just as Marine spymaster Maj. Pete Ellis did to predict the Japanese expansion across the Pacific and our eventual war with them—20 years before the fact; a neat trick—the gathering of information is critical to the flyfisher who wishes to probe the depths of a lake with his fly. This is where every flyfisher must begin if he is to succeed on a regular basis. He must gather information beforehand and throughout his foray.

There are three primary methods for determining what the bottom structure is like.

Sonar

One day I found myself aboard a submarine, the USS *Barbel*, apparently about a million fathoms (a fathom is Navy talk for 6 feet) below the surface of the Pacific. I was making a nuisance of myself on the bridge by asking questions, one of which was directed to a sailor who had a headset on and was punching buttons on what was then a state-of-the-art computer keyboard. He was a sonarman and

If you are going to spend more than a few dollars on tackle, then spend a few more on a depth finder.

appeared to know everything about the bottom below and the water around the sub that could possibly be known. He showed me very technical and detailed depictions of the bottom and things that were in or on the surface of the water, including another submarine, ledges, rocks, trenches, a volcano, mountains, plains, whales, and sundry other things. I was impressed.

Walking back to the forward torpedo room where members of my team were sharpening their knives, I contemplated this thing called sonar, which the sailor had told me means sound navigation and ranging. I wondered if it could be used to catch more fish.

Today, affordable and quite accurate sonar sets known as depth and fish finders decorate many fishing boats, particularly those belonging to bass and trout anglers who troll a great deal. Surprisingly few flyfishers, on the other hand, use these devices to fish lakes. I am not certain why this is, but I suspect that most flyfishers shy away from fish finders because they see such electronics as little use to them. This is unfortunate.

The development of more practical and efficient sink-tip and full-sink lines, and the refinement of flies that can now get to the bottom and stay there, has made the bottom an eminently more fishable place than, say, 30 years ago when I began flyfishing. Because of these developments, fish finders are most definitely useful tools, for not only can the flyfisher so equipped see what the bottom structure is like (and whether there are any fish holding in and on it), he can now access that structure with relative ease.

Nevertheless, many flyfishers still won't go near a fish finder because it is a piece of high-tech gear that, to them, represents an unfair advantage over their

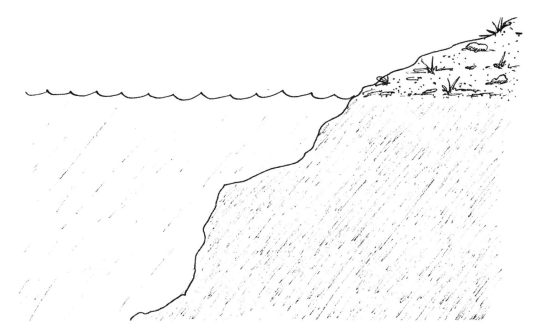

This cross section reflects how the terrain on shore can be continued into the water.

quarry. They think these thoughts while holding a $500 fly reel machined to extreme precision that is attached to a $600 fly rod designed with the same technology used to build a Trident submarine, arguably the most advanced piece of hardware in existence. The contradiction is obvious.

If you are serious about catching more fish on the fly, you should use a fish finder. Heresy? Certainly. But A.J. McClane and Lee Wulff were also considered heretics by many when they began pushing their catch-and-release philosophy, and we see where that got us.

Topographic and Lake Maps

A topographic map is a two-dimensional depiction of the earth's surface that shows relief (the lay of the land) and elevation (height above mean sea level). It also shows "cultural" features such as roads, fences, bridges, buildings, and so on, as well as vegetation. So what good are topo maps to the flyfisher?

North America is covered with man-made lakes, ponds, and reservoirs that were once fields, farms, roads, valleys, gravel pits, quarries, and other types of countryside. When these features are submerged, everything on the surface of the land becomes structure, which can still be located by using a topo map.

Although there is always a potential drawback to using such a map—in this case the fact that the map may be somewhat out of date and therefore may not reflect every feature, since someone could have built a barn the day after the data for the map was compiled—topo maps represent an excellent source of information when putting flies to bottom structure. Likewise, some municipalities offer lake maps that show bottom configuration.

The riprap on this bank continues into the water at this angle for a few feet, and then the bottom levels out.

This dirt bank carries right into the water at this angle for about 30 feet.

It takes a bit of practice to read a topo map accurately, especially when the "ground" you are trying to locate is now underwater. The answer is to use terrain association, which in this instance is matching the terrain you can see surrounding the water with that represented on the map, and then biangulating or triangulating between obvious terrain features to place yourself over a certain piece of structure in the water. You can make this more accurate by using a depth finder to find objects on the bottom that match those on the map.

Terrain Continuance

As we will learn in the chapter on saltwater river structure, it is often possible to deduce what the bottom of a small lake or pond consists of by looking at the

nearby terrain. In many cases, that terrain reflects what the bottom adjacent to it is like. For instance, banks lining a reservoir that are covered with stumps right up to the water's edge are likely to be carried on right into the water.

Of course, one can always use scuba or snorkeling gear to dive down and find out firsthand what the bottom is like, but this can usually be avoided by using the techniques discussed above.

OPEN THE REFRIGERATOR

The bottom of a lake can be likened to a refrigerator; it is a place where a large amount of fresh food exists nearly all of the time. Fish know this, especially smallmouth bass, bream, and trout, which explains why they get such a large percentage of their forage from and around the bottom.

Details, Details

To master the refrigerator, you must first have a sound working knowledge of the gamefish and forage that live there. You must understand why, when, and how your quarry eats thereabouts, and you must have the correct tackle and know-how to use it. You must also be intimately familiar with the appearance and behavior of your quarry's quarry, and that might be quite some list of potential victims. It takes study and a willingness to ponder what to others seems like minutiae. For instance, madtoms (*Noturus*) are believed by most anglers to exist solely in rivers, streams, creeks, and occasionally their backwaters. But at least three species of madtom—the stonecat (*Noturus flavus*), brindled madtom (*Noturus miurus*), and tadpole madtom (*Noturus gyrinus*)—can be found in lakes where smallmouth bass dwell.

As discussed further in Chapter 9 (Freshwater Stream and River Structure), predatory fish like smallmouths hunt along the bottom because 1) it is easier for them to catch prey there, and 2) that prey is abundant because of the structure the bottom represents. An abundance of prey species and ease of foraging are two critical factors in determining what structure holds more gamefish. (Equally important is how predators can pin prey against the bottom.)

Bottom structure in lakes ranges from gravel and detritus from trees to rocks, ledges, drop-offs, and myriad other anomalies. Microscopic life forms the foundation of structure, even on gravel bottoms that have little else to offer but the gravel itself, and it is that life that attracts slightly larger things that feed on it, such as scuds and insect larvae. In turn, small fish feed on the smallest of these, and on up the food chain. The flyfisher must never assume that a lack of profound structure on a lake bottom equates to an equally profound lack of gamefish. It just isn't the case.

A gravel bar in shallow water amid sparse bulrushes.

But your approach to such structure requires an understanding of how game-fish feed on it. The difference between how trout, smallmouth, and bream forage on minor, as opposed to major, structure is in their approach. Here they are much more transient, preferring to slowly cruise over the structure and eat what they come upon rather than hold on or in structure and hunt by ambush those species that fail to detect them hiding there. Adding to this equation is how even a predator feels vulnerable when exposed to open spaces like a gravel bottom with no other structure to speak of. This undoubtedly helps to keep the gamefish moving, lest it itself become a quick meal for something like a pike or muskellunge.

In this situation, numerous repeated casts to the gravel bottom are called for. This puts and keeps your fly, which should be kept on or within a few inches of the bottom (a Clouser Deep Minnow is undoubtedly one of the best flies here for smallies, with a bead-head Gold-ribbed Hare's Ear, Prince nymph, or Pheasant Tail being excellent for trout and bream), in the strike zone—a necessity when casting to fish on the move. Remember that, as alluded to earlier in this chapter, your line and leader must work in harmony with the fly, meaning that it must be heavy enough to help keep the fly down. There are few things more frustrating than not being able to keep a fly down on the bottom when you know that's where the fish are.

Taylor Streit, a well-known flyfishing guide in northern New Mexico, is considered by many in the region to be the master at working weighted nymphs just above the bottom of ranch ponds like that of the Blackfire Flyfishing Guest Ranch in Angel Fire. He uses a pretty fast, long-sink-tip line and usually a weighted or bead-head nymph like a Pheasant Tail or Gold-ribbed Hare's Ear to get at the largest rainbows and cutts in the pond, which are most often found more near the bottom than close to the surface.

Another often undervalued and sometimes overlooked factor to consider when working flies along the bottom is the fly's action. I believe that gamefish being tempted with streamers and nymphs tend to focus more on the fly's movement than precise color pattern and shape, which is unlike fishing a dry. Will Ryan, in his excellent *Smallmouth Strategies for the Fly Rod* (New York: Lyons & Burford, 1996) points this out and cites the same thoughts of Bob Clouser and Harry Murray, and I couldn't agree more. When you fish bottom structure, your fly often needs only to act like forage rather than be a exact replica of the primary forage there. Matching the proverbial hatch is far less often a factor.

And what of rods for fishing the bottom of lakes? I am of the opinion that there is seldom a need to go any heavier than a 7-weight. I say this because you will not be throwing large, wind-resistant poppers and deer-hair bugs tight against rocks on the surface, flies that have to be sent flying by the rod and line and then turned over by the leader. You will instead be casting small to mid-sized streamers and nymphs that don't require the force a heavy popper does and that comparatively seldom have to be sent into those tight quarters. A 6- or 7-weight rod 8 1/2 to 9 feet long with a medium-fast action will almost always suffice. Naturally, fishing a wind-blown high-plains lake like those in eastern Wyoming might require a heavier rod if casting large flies. Adapt.

STRUCTURE SPECIFICS

At this point we should examine some specifics of structure you might encounter on the bottom of a lake.

Rocks, Rock Piles, Sunken Islands, Bars, and Humps

From a standpoint of open water and the bottom structure it presents, rocks, rock piles, sunken islands, and humps present the flyfisher with some of the most delightful action. With the possible exception of a channel cut in the bottom or a ledge, these natural fish magnets offer more opportunities than all other types of bottom structure. The reason is isolation.

More than just havens for the smallmouths of summer, these types of structure offer feeding grounds for lake trout (togue), walleye, crappie, bluegills, northern pike, muskellunge, largemouths, landlocked stripers, wipers (a white bass-and-striper combo), and white bass, to name a handful. This kind of structure provides cover to terrified baitfish in an otherwise wide-open expanse of water and in doing so draws gamefish and concentrates them in one area. Isolated structure of this kind is never to be overlooked.

Your casts should begin on the outside edges and work their way in toward the center of the structure, and you must work the entire circumference. This methodi-

Generally speaking, a single log off by itself, especially in clear waters like those in the top and middle photos won't hold as many fish as a jumble of logs in ever so slightly stained waters, as those in the bottom photo.

78

cal approach allows you to pick up fish on the outside so that a struggling fish isn't brought out past other fish, which are likely to spook. It also allows you to be thorough in your coverage. If there is one mistake flyfishers make more often than others when working structure like this, it is not covering all the available structure slowly and thoroughly.

In Maine's Knox County there resides Seven Tree Pond, into which flows the St. George River. Where the river wanes and the pond begins, a large boulder and several lesser rocks rest on the bottom. As the ice vanishes into the persistent spring, browns gather here to partake of the many rainbow smelt making their way up the river to spawn. These browns hide among the rocks and dash out to capture the darting smelt, which makes this location especially productive at this time of year. Flies cast among the rocks and fading current find plentiful targets, true, but flies cast 20 or more feet short of these rocks go ignored, for the browns are not there—the area offers very little structure in which to hide.

Above: Also, do be sure that the log you are casting to is in fact a log; there are impersonators out there.

Left: The author working a log at the base of flooded saplings. (Susan Newman photo.)

79

If you cross the north end of the pond heading east toward South Union, you will see a casket mill. To the left of the mill is a small, nameless stream that empties into Seven Tree, and in front of the confluence about 40 feet out is a gravel bar. Between the gravel bar and the stream's mouth is slack, deeper water. Browns wait in this slack water for the smelt to enter and attempt to gain a purchase in the stream on their way up to Crawford Pond in the highlands above, but many never make it. The trout chase the smelt up against the gravel bar and eat their fill.

These two examples show how the flyfisher must study structure to determine how the gamefish there are using it to their advantage.

Ledges, Drop-Offs, and Channels

Sudden inclines are the common factor with ledges, drop-offs, and channels in the lake bottom. Even if there is minimal supporting structure, such as vegetation, marked changes in the slope of the bottom draw fish for no other reason than they are there. It's the old adage: why did you climb the mountain? Because it is there. Thus: why did you go to the drop-off? You got it.

The bottom of Maine's Alford Lake in Hope has a trench running down it. I know this because I spoke with the pilot of a minisub who went down there many years ago searching for the body of an angler who had come up missing. The pilot said that many, many large landlocked salmon were gathered in this trench, all of which were far bigger than those regularly caught by fishermen. Sadly, these salmon, so long as they stay down in that trench, are safe from flyfishers, for the depth thereabouts is somewhere around 90 feet. But the point is clear.

Only about a 10-minute drive from Alford is Crawford Pond in the town of Union. The deep water that runs from Salmon Point down toward where the old rock bridge used to be is abutted by drop-offs and ledges that are very accessible to the flyfisher, and the large browns that spend much of their time in the deepest holes do sometimes rise from their shadowed world to feed along these drop-offs and ledges. Streamers (Kennebago Smelt, Gray Ghost, Nine-Three, Warden's Worry, and Mickey Finn) fished at night around this structure are often attacked by these hungry browns.

Submerged Logs

When you bring up the subject of logs, many folks picture catfish. But there are plenty of other species to be found on such structure, including bream, northern pike, stripers, white bass, muskellunge, largemouth bass, walleye, lake trout, grayling, and a host of others.

Logs hold fish in the traditional sense, that being that most fish will hold or "suspend" above the log, but they usually hold somewhat tighter than, say, smallies suspending over rocks.

Because they were once on land, logs forming bottom structure are often in shallow enough water to be seen. If you can see the log, then any fish holding on it can likely see you. This is where many flyfishers go wrong; they make too close an approach. Instead of getting right up close to see whether there is anything on the log—and it is often impossible to see any fish holding on the log, anyway, unless the water is very clear—stand off and make as long a cast as possible. You will probably only have to make one or two casts to cover the log because most gamefish holding there will be able to see your fly from wherever they are on the log. Obviously, in murky water you will want to make a few extra casts just to be sure.

Begin by casting to spots well away from the log and work your way in toward it. Many fish hold on logs: trout, smallmouth and largemouth bass, and northern pike, to name a few.

Chapter 6

Saltwater Shoreline Structure

One of the greatest forms of saltwater shoreline structure: the famous arch at Cabo San Lucas, Baja.

The bristly snout of the manatee slips beneath the gray surface as we silently approach the petite canal on Florida's Banana River Lagoon. Black-mangroves line the right side and back of the canal, perhaps 50 feet from end to end. A small dock almost wholly swallowed up by the feisty trees and their tentacled, hooplike roots helps to form the northern edge.

Richard Jee is in the bow and places a cast just beyond the old dock. Instantly his rod bends heavily, but the phantom fish is gone just as quickly. We see it flee past our boat, a great streak of silver bent for the lagoon and some unseen haven. Perhaps the largest spotted seatrout I have ever seen, I estimate the fish's weight at 12 pounds.

Another cast to the same spot and this time the take holds. A few moments later a brilliant "speck" shines in Richard's hand and is then delivered back to its lair. But the phantom is gone, bent for points south.

An hour later we spy the great fish again, this time in a tiny grotto beside an island our guide tells us is man-made. The fish fools with our offering, but then departs in haste as he did earlier.

In another quiet canal where mottled ducks cavort and whirl overhead, the phantom is seen yet again, this time not waiting for anything we might have to

83

proffer. As it races by the boat I am sure the fish is the heaviest I have ever encountered, and I have caught many seatrout, from the Bogue Banks to Boca Grande.

Then I realize that this isn't one fish at all, but three different trout. My mind grinds to a halt with this astonishing realization. Two years earlier such a revelation would have set the local fishing community on its ear, but then there was the celebrated net ban, and today the lagoon is teeming with seatrout, and these three are now but a commonplace trio among many. A rare and splendid victory, one I savor with particular relish, for it is was on these very waters that I took my first spotted seatrout 25 years earlier.

Manatee

Back in the first canal, all the trout are stacked on the right-hand side and toward the back, ignoring the structure on the left side, which appears equally appealing to our apparently unknowing eyes. The sun is directly overhead, and there is no wind in the canal, making light and wind non sequiturs. Then the dim of my gray matter is pierced with a shaft of brilliant light, and I realize that the baitfish in the lagoon are afforded much more cover in the labyrinth of oyster-encrusted mangrove roots than the spartan cover of the dock and boat tied to it, so much so that they totally avoid the other side of the canal. This tidbit of information arrived with a delay because I was still thinking in terms of the saltwater shoreline structure I last fished, that being the innumerable docks of the Atlantic Intracoastal Waterway around the fishing village of Swansboro. There, docks are excellent structure for trout—as they are in other canals along the Banana River Lagoon, but not this one—for they provide places to hide for what is surely millions of baitfish amid the terror of predators like the fanged seatrout, murderous crevalle jack, and giant tarpon, among others.

My delay in understanding why all the trout were gathered on the edges of the canal that sported mangrove roots was one many flyfishers make; they assume that structure that holds fish on one water will do the same everywhere else similar structure is encountered, but nothing could be less correct.

IT'S THE SAME THING, ONLY DIFFERENT

That is the best way to describe two types of saltwater shoreline structure; it's the same thing, only different. I suspect I first learned this maxim as a lad working the shoreline rocks of the St. George River in Thomaston, Maine, where there patrolled a great many striped bass. This was back in the 1960s, 15 years before the striper crash of the 80s, and the mysterious waters of the "narrows" below the foreboding Maine State Prison—an institution I suspect my parents, teachers, neighbors, and fellow hoodlums assumed would one day be my address—were known for giving up some massive stripers. But I quickly learned that the rocks forming the shoreline thereabouts would hold stripers one day and be void of them the next; an annoying and perplexing poser that I promised myself I would one day decipher. It took me some years, but I did eventually fulfill that promise.

The answer to the riddle lay in the transient nature of the fish that call saltwater shoreline structure home. Of all the types of structure in all the waters of the earth, it is that which forms the edges of the saltwater world that is most transitory, for this is a realm of tides and energy and perpetual motion and death. Determining what fish will be where when in this treacherous world is, therefore, the greatest challenge a flyfisher can accept. Even the old masters—Kreh, Apte, Sosin, Fernandez—admit to spending much of their lives trying to solve the puzzle that is the saltwater shoreline, and most still say that they have yet to declare total

Above: A spotted seatrout caught working a spartina bank.

Left: Spartina marshes can form their own shorelines.

victory. And, of course, they never will, for the moment they did a situation would arise that bewildered them, and the game would begin anew, for this is the nature of flyfishing.

Let's go back to the mangroves.

MANGROVES

Of all saltwater shoreline structure, mangroves are perhaps the most intricate. The most common mangrove in North America is the black-mangrove (*Avicennia germinans*), which is a member of the Verbena family (*Verbenaceae*), a

Mangrove roots.

86

complex, very successful family (3,000 species) that consist of everything from large trees to shrubs, vines, and even herbs. There are three other species of mangroves in North America, with southern Florida playing host to them all, but the black-mangrove is the one we must concern ourselves with, for it is this tree that can be found from east central Florida around the tip of the state and on to the Texas Gulf Coast.

Residents In Waiting

Mangroves in Florida harbor an impressive list of resident gamefish: tarpon, snook, spotted seatrout, red drum, black drum, crevalle jacks, mangrove (gray) snapper, and many others. One might think that, given this, mangroves would mean that one can motor right up to them and begin catching fish like there was no tomorrow and not much left of today, but that isn't always the case. As with any structure, sometimes the fish are there in abundance and are ready to jump on whatever you bless them with. Other times it seems as if nothing will do the trick.

Upper left: Snook. (Capt. Les Hill photo.)

Far left: Spotted seatrout. (Capt. Les Hill photo.)

Left: Red drum. (Capt. Les Hill photo.)

The answer lies in being able to decipher individual mangrove groves and determine what gamefish are hidden among the roots. Simply because those roots can hold several species of gamefish doesn't mean those roots are holding gamefish, and no species feeds all the time.

A peek into the water beneath some mangroves is itself a revelation. The roots of the tree and surrounding water are usually filled with life, from the smallest plankton and marine invertebrates to enormous tarpon, scrappy snook, rugged little mangrove snapper, and seemingly infinite more gamefish and baitfish. But not all mangroves are created equal, at least not in the eyes of selective gamefish.

The best mangroves are those that offer

— deep water both far back into the maze of roots and close to the leading edge of the roots so that an attack can be short and swift;

— a strong current that carries baitfish like finger mullet, menhaden, and glass minnows past the roots where trouble lies in wait; and

— abundant shade that allows gamefish to get out of the sun and lurk in shadows from which they will strike.

The best way to size up some mangroves is to observe them quietly from a short distance away. What can you see and hear? Does it appear as though the water remains deep well back into the tangle of roots? Are there some deep-water cuts nearby that gamefish can use safely to come and go from the roots? Is there a strong tidal flow (a full moon can be a tremendous boon)? Can you hear or see fish feeding? Are there baitfish skittering about in apparent fright? Are the mangroves thick enough to provide good shade?

These are just some of the factors you must consider if you are going to fully exploit mangroves, and one of the best locations to study mangroves is in Belize. At the invitation of owners Marguerite Miles and Mike Heusner, I spent several days fishing the mangroves of Belize from the Belize River Lodge in February of 1998. This beautiful lodge offers the flyfisher the chance to fish the famous red mangrove "cathedral" on Haulover Creek, with its gigantic roots and substantial population of snook, tarpon, crevalle jack, and mangrove snapper, as well as the other species of mangroves out in the cays.

It is quickly made clear to the flyfisher, by shrewd guides like Martin and Pedro, that you simply must be able to get your fly very tight to the roots if you want to consistently catch fish. With the overhanging branches, an accurate side-cast is required in many situations. Indentations in the root line and points are excellent targets.

When the fish hits, you must put the rod to the fish and get it away from those roots quickly. Deceivers, Stu Aptes, and Cockroaches are all excellent, even on the snapper, which are my favorite gamefish in the mangrove roots of Belize.

The red man-
grove "cathe-
dral" on
Haulover Creek.

A derelict tug
lies at one end of
the "cathedral"
and is home to
rugged snook.

89

Above: Martin, a seasoned guide at the Belize River Lodge, prepares a leader on Black Creek.

Above right: This handsome snapper jumped the author's tarpon fly within two inches of the roots. (Peder Lund photo.)

Right: Young snappers and other fish hold tight to the mangrove roots at the southern tip of Long Cay, Belize.

90

Seasonal Solutions

Flyfishers who have figured out the mangroves all have a keen understanding of how seasonal changes affect gamefish behavior, which of course is greatly affected by baitfish behavior. Decipher how and why these changes take place and you will substantially increase your success among the mangrove roots.

Winter

Mangroves are places of great change, which is best demonstrated with the coming of winter. There can be excellent fishing spring through fall, but winter is often the best time to get far back up a mangrove-lined canal to seek out the snook and other gamefish that gather there to take advantage of the warmest water they can find. Both snook and tarpon are fish of the tropics and subtropics, which means that water temperatures below the 60s will not be tolerated for very long at all, and can even kill. Certain species of baitfish also prefer warmer water, so they too pile into shallow, sunny canals that are protected from the wind by mangroves during the winter months. The flyfisher who can get back into these places often finds himself surrounded by hungry fish willing to attack any fly cast to them.

But canals lined with mangroves, by their very nature, do not lend themselves to easy battles once the fish is hooked. Quite the contrary. I suspect that more inshore gamefish are broken off on mangrove roots than most other types of structure, with pilings being a top contender in that realm. The flyfisher must remember and always keep in mind that the same roots the gamefish used as cover to set an ambush can be used for retreat, and powerful fish like tarpon and snook are masters at regaining a purchase in the oyster- and barnacle-encrusted roots of mangroves.

The situation calls for a stiff rod and the nerve to use it. If you watch professional guides like Boca Grande's Capt. Richard Hyland, Charlotte Harbor's Capt. Les Hill, Key West's Capt. Steven Lamp, and the Indian River Lagoon's Capt. Rodney Smith, you will see them putting great pressure to a fish once it is hooked near mangrove roots. They use abrasion-resistant leaders and constantly put pressure on the fish to wear it out quickly. If the fish is swimming to the left, the pressure is applied to the right, and vice versa. They have figured out how to not be intimidated, as so many flyfishers are, when a fish is running and jumping; at the first opportunity, they use the rod to exert what most flyfishers would consider far too much force on the fish in the opposite direction of which it is traveling, and they keep that pressure on, never allowing the fish to have a chance at wrapping the leader or line around a root.

Spring

Spring is a time of great wonder in the mangroves. At no time of the year is it more clear just how important mangroves are to the hatching and rearing of juvenile baitfish and gamefish.

91

Mangroves in the spring can be likened to the asphalt outside Manhattan's Orvis New York, Holland & Holland, Urban Angler, and Hunting World at the height of the lunch hour, with back alleys, sidewalks, main thoroughfares, crosswalks, and side streets all filled to capacity as everyone rushes about. It's a numbers game. For instance, a single female tarpon can give birth to nearly 20 million larvae, of which perhaps 1 percent survive the first month and a half of life. Born in the open ocean, the new tarpon go through a metamorphosis from an eel-like form to something more like a fish. They then migrate inshore and seek out quiet, low-energy backwaters preferably lined with mangroves, which afford the vulnerable youngsters some measure of protection. With hundreds of thousands of female tarpon around south Florida, the numbers quickly add up. Throw all the other gamefish into the equation—seatrout, snook, ladyfish, flounder, redfish, jacks, and so on—and then toss in baitfish, which are, naturally, more abundant than the gamefish, and you begin to see why backwater mangroves are so dynamic come spring.

All these young fish seek mangrove waters that are out of the way, difficult to access, and less than perfect (in the eyes of the adult gamefish) because fewer large gamefish must be worried about. Therefore, mangroves with minimal strong tidal flows and little deep water back in the roots and adjacent to or in front of the root line are less appealing to the bigger gamefish and more so to the little guys. Given this, the largest gamefish won't be found hereabouts nearly as often as they will at intercept points between inlets and these backwater nurseries.

Spring being a time of plenty, the flyfisher must be especially watchful for opportunities that allow him to present a fly in such a way that a gamefish will have a more difficult time turning it down. Gamefish can afford to be more selective during this time of year, with what are often literally hundreds of baitfish in view at any one time, and a staggering assortment of them at that: in southern Florida alone there are five species of silversides (tidewater, reef, hardhead, inland, and rough; a sixth species, the key silverside, is found in the lower Keys); six primary species of mullet (liza, striped, mountain, fantail, white, and redeye, the latter of which is especially abundant in and around mangroves); at least a dozen species of herring (the little-eye, dwarf, shortband, and Atlantic thread herring; Gulf and yellowfin menhaden; false pilchard; Spanish, orangespot, redear, and scaled sardine; and the threadfin shad); six species of anchovy (flat, bigeye, Cuban, dusky, bay, and silver); and many others such as pinfish (a type of porgy) and needlefish. Now bring in crustaceans (primarily shrimp and crabs) and mollusks and you can see why the very best fly and presentation is often necessary to continually hook up with the largest, most experienced gamefish. It is of no consequence that not all the aforementioned species of baitfish inhabit mangroves, but all in some way come into contact with the gamefish that know certain prey species are making their way to and from mangroves.

I believe there are three primary approaches the flyfisher can take to entice gamefish that have their pick of prey in this time of superabundance.

One approach is to present a fly that appears to be something different and unusual; something not seen every day. This tactic can be compared with the pitcher's change-up pitch, which often gets a recalcitrant batter to swing at a pitch that he normally would not. This is a modified version of the principle behind flies like the Royal Coachman and Mickey Finn, which imitate no species in particular but which catch many gamefish every year.

Another approach is to present a fly that appears to be badly wounded and in need of immediate dispatching, a tack that takes advantage of the gamefish's instinctive reaction to kill and eat prey that is easy to catch and that promises a substantial meal, meaning that a large fly should be used.

The third approach is to work the structure again and again, casting and casting over and over into each likely looking spot until rewarded with a strike. This approach is used on autumn landlocked salmon that have become complacent after feeding heavily all spring and summer, and it can work just as well in the spring mangroves.

Summer

Mangroves are plants of subtropical and tropical shallows, meaning that water temperatures in the dead of summer can reach and surpass the upper temperature range of many gamefish, such as tarpon, which prefer water between 75 and 85 degrees for optimal metabolism. One answer to this is to find the deepest cuts near the mangroves, where gamefish can take up position in the cooler deep water to await prey moving to and from the mangroves with the tide. Red drum, ladyfish, snook, seatrout, jacks, and a host of others can be readily found in these haunts, as can assorted snapper and even grouper. Another answer is to work areas with minimal direct sunlight that are also exposed to the wind. Fronts bringing slightly cooler temperatures with them are also exploitable, and mangroves with lighter bottoms tend to hold heat less efficiently, bringing water temps down a bit from nearby areas with darker bottoms.

Gamefish hanging around mangroves in summer can be coaxed into action by exploiting their sense of smell and their instinctive reaction to other gamefish feeding, even if those others are smaller than they are. An excellent way to pull this off is to toss three or four small handfuls of chum and the occasional live bait into an area with a current running past it. Do not overdo it; a few small handfuls and a teaser once in a while is what's called for, not a huge chum block and dozens of finger mullet tossed in because the old adage of "the more, the merrier" seems applicable. Also, although considered heresy by some, a liquid fish attractant applied to the fly can seriously change gamefish attitude in a hurry. It should be mentioned here, however, that the International Game Fish Association

Baitfish like these pinfish (spottail pinfish on the bottom) are fed upon heavily by large seatrout.

(IGFA) will disallow any potential record fish if it was taken on a fly that had attractant applied.

Fall

Many guides who work mangroves prefer autumn fishing because of the tremendous change in the attitude of many gamefish. Fish, like all animals, are affected by seasonal changes, and autumn is a time of preparation and anxiety for gamefish, although they do not realize that what is driving them to feed heavily is the innate knowledge that they must prepare for the coming winter and a sense that if they don't, they will perish.

The gamefish of autumn tend to be larger on average because they have had the opportunity to feed well since spring. But this does not mean that every flyfisher will have wonderful results on each outing. The key is to locate, anticipate, and present interesting flies in places where the largest fish are more likely to be. This means you must know the species you are targeting very well. Otherwise, you are taking shots in the dark.

Take seatrout, for example. On a flat you will usually find that the specks are all the same size or darn close to it. This isn't the case in the mangroves, where one speck might be 12 inches long and the one 6 feet away twice that length. I don't know why this is, but it is a truth any experienced speck guide or angler will tell you.

Since the gamefish of autumn are larger on average, it is often advisable to use larger flies. The maxim of "throw larger flies for larger fish" rings true, especially in this instance.

Also, target potential lies that appear to have no baitfish swimming near them. There may well be a reason why no baitfish are there, and it might be a hungry trophy snook, tarpon, or speck that is being avoided at all costs.

Finally, upgrade your leader somewhat and make sure that there are no nicks

in it or the fly line; we wouldn't want to be accused of not using enough "gun" or not taking the time to continually check our tackle for signs of trouble.

DOCKS, PIERS, AND SEA WALLS

Some of the very best saltwater shoreline structure was put there by man; a most unexpected and pleasant situation given his oftentimes ruinous tendencies when it comes to his environment. Nevertheless, the fact remains that docks, piers, jetties, and similar shoreline structure helping to form the edges of our inshore salt waters provide the flyfisher with what is often some of the best fishing available. Better yet, this structure is often right in our own front yards or at least within a double haul's distance away.

Capt. Rodney Smith and I were working a sea wall and a small dock from his flats boat in the Banana River near Cocoa Beach. We had been taking redfish in the 35-pound range, but conditions in the afternoon had put the fish down, so we switched from reds to specks and whatever else was hungry. It didn't take long for the action to pick up again.

The water along the sea wall and dock was shallow—no more than 3 feet

Red drum.
(Capt. Rodney
Smith photo.)

95

deep. With weighted flies on floating lines we cast at a slight angle toward the wall and let the flies settle to the bottom before beginning a series of short strips. There is a trench at the base of the wall formed by wave action against it, and in that trench were several mangrove snapper—nothing big, but feisty and colorful juveniles that hit with gumption and gave a good show of themselves. We caught several before they wised up and got lockjaw.

In the narrow canal around the corner from the sea wall there is a small dock and some old cypress knees. It was quiet back in there, and we were concerned that the sea cow we startled, which blew out in a tremendous swirl of water and mud, had spooked the trout that we suspected were hiding in the shade of the dock and beneath the overhanging cypress branches draped with Spanish moss.

Rodney tied on one of his 2/0 Schroach patterns and put the fly right beneath the dock. It disappeared in the shadow and was instantly inhaled by a brilliant 2-pound speck that bent Rodney's rod nicely. The IGFA record-holding and producing guide stripped the pretty fish in and quickly released it as my line went tight with pressure from another speck that was hiding behind a cypress knee in a big patch of shade. Eight trout in all came out of that small space no longer than a fly line and about as wide as a leader is long used on the most skittish Madison trout, and they were all tight on the structure of the dock and cypress knees covered with shade. We couldn't buy a speck out in the sunlit channel where "personal watercraft" and an endless parade of water-skiers buzzed around with screams of glee.

In the evening, after supper, I walked out onto the pier beside a big boathouse on Patrick Air Force Base. The pier turns into a sea wall at the end, which bends around to form a completely protected little bay of sorts, and the boathouse itself was elevated on pilings with about 3 feet between the surface and the bottom of the building (the boathouse is gone now but the pilings are still there).

The sun was setting in a spectacular display over the river as I worked the 2/0 gray-on-white Clouser along the pilings of the boathouse, pier, and sea wall. The specks went stupid, eating the soon-to-be-mangled Clouser as if they had never seen such a thing before. One after another up to 5 pounds.

Every fish we caught that afternoon and evening was in very close proximity to docks, pilings, cypress knees, and sea walls—but only on the sides of the structure facing the protected water; there were none on the more choppy side—and all were interested in shade; no fish were feeding in the open. The lesson was reinforced a few months later while fishing the Atlantic Intracoastal Waterway near the North Carolina village of Swansboro. This area of the waterway has many large houses with boat docks and many other types of structure, including spartina beds rife with oysters, flats and drop-offs, a deep channel, sloughs, coves, bridge pilings, and so on.

It was a hot July afternoon, the North Carolina sun beating down on the water. The humidity was typically high. The water temperature was 83 degrees and there wasn't a breath of air. Finger mullet, glass minnows, and innumerable juvenile menhaden were everywhere, skittering across the surface as unseen predators struck at them from below. From time to time a lizardfish would attack the baitfish and could be seen spinning wildly above the surface, its long, brown, snakelike body plopping back into the water.

With bright sunshine, high temps, lots of boat traffic, and plenty of forage available, I believed that the specks and drum would be staying out of the busy channel and out of the sun, ambushing meals from the shade and quiet safety of the docks.

Bend Backs, Clousers, and swimming crab imitations did the trick, with dozens of "puppy" drum (a North Carolina term for juvenile red drum) and specks to 3 pounds pouncing on the offerings. Every cast that produced a fish put the fly within a foot of the dock on the shady side. Nothing was interested in anything farther away, and there was no activity on the flats or in the channel, despite baitfish being everywhere.

When gamefish feel pressure from the elements— in this case the sun, high temps, and cavorting plea-

Above: The author with a mediocre Banana River Lagoon red drum. (Rick Pelow photo.)

Left: The author checks dock pilings along Long Cay in Belize. (Peder Lund photo.)

97

Right: Barnacle-encrusted pilings on Florida's Banana River Lagoon.

Inset: Capt. Rodney Smith works a fly tight to some pilings. Note the low rod tip, which is directly aligned with the line in preparation for a strip strike.

sure boaters—they will seek out structure that affords them relief and, if available, a place from which to ambush bait. The obvious is often just that because it truly is a likely place for the gamefish to be.

But to be especially effective you must also consider the direction of the current and what structure the fish have to lie behind. That afternoon along the waterway I found that the fish would only hold under docks that had shade on the down-current side. This allowed the fish to face into the current while holding behind a piling and still remain in the shade. They had everything they wanted beneath some docks; less attractive docks held substantially fewer fish, and those were always smaller than the fish under the "best" docks. Another thing I noticed was that the drum wanted only crab imitations presented as swimming crabs drifting by on the surface with the current. At one point I stopped fishing and caught one of the live swimming crabs going by the boat. I maneuvered about 20 feet up-current from a dock with lots of shade and some thick pilings on the down-current

A dock with pilings, current, and shade.

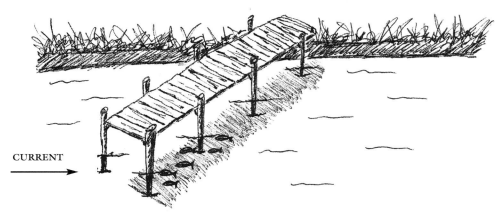

CURRENT

side and dropped the crab in the water. The current took the creature within a foot of the outside piling and the crustacean disappeared in a heavy swoosh, the fat drum gulping the free meal as soon as it saw it. (Note here that the drum were feeding on the surface rather than along the bottom, their usual tack.)

Atlantic Beach, North Carolina, guide Capt. Bill Harris points out an interesting fact about the interrelationship between docks, birds, and red drum. He notes that docks with birds perched on them seldom have drum beneath them because of the drum's knowledge of the birds' equaling danger. The drum actually look for the birds and avoid docks where they perch. Keep this in mind when working docks.

The most successful flyfishers pay special attention to the little details of docks, pilings, piers, and sea walls, knowing that one will hold fish and another won't because the former has exactly what the fish need and the latter doesn't. They also know that some situations find gamefish hiding as far as possible from noisy waters, yet other situations find them just far enough away from the bedlam to give them an acceptable sense of safety and comfort.

CULVERTS

Spending some of my youth growing up in south and central Florida, I was

99

exposed to many flyfishing situations. Many days were spent studying structure, from the docks lining the Intracoastal Waterway around Ft. Lauderdale and the old canals in and around what was then Sunrise Golf Village to the backwaters of the Indian River Lagoon and the warren of mosquito-control ditches of St. Lucie County. It was the latter where I found many young tarpon hiding in the 285 miles of ditches that were first conceived in the mid-1920s and completed about 10 years later. Quite a few of those tarpon were found hanging around the culverts that link the various ditches, the Indian River Lagoon, and assorted backwaters, and I soon found myself seeking out overgrown ditches with culverts with regularity.

Although the tarpon were abundant around the culverts (still are), it was seldom easy to get at them, and once gotten at, the challenge of keeping one on was considerable. This was because the ditches were oftentimes lined with all manner of vegetation, from brush and Spanish bayonet to tall grass and a bevy of thorny shrubs. Mangroves were also out in force. Throw in bothersome snakes like the Eastern diamondback rattler and add a cranky 'gator or two (two critters that have the annoying habit of remaining very still and unseen until you are much too close), and you begin to see why the tarpon would go largely unmolested by flyfishers. But I was never accused of being especially bright as a boy, so I would just poke at the snakes and 'gators with the tip of my fly rod to get them to loiter elsewhere, and the ditch would temporarily be mine.

Of course, there was the time in 1967 when the game warden had to be called to the overgrown canal behind the Mueller's house on NW 17th Court in Sunrise, this because Jeff Browning and I had unsuccessfully attempted to get the big 'gator to leave by depositing the entire contents of our respective fathers' tackle boxes on the back, sides, and tail of the overgrown lizard. Realizing too late that retired police officer Bill Newman and current Florida Highway Patrolman Mr. Browning would take a dim view of the gator going through life with dozens of their lures and flies attached to its hide, we called the warden and informed him that the 'gator was being bad and may in fact have eaten several neighborhood children (we hadn't seen Ronny Bright that day, after all, nor Jeff's sister Lorraine). The young warden showed up with his beautiful blonde wife, both of whom promptly rowed a johnboat over to the basking 'gator and piled onto him. (Listen, I have a neighborhood full of witnesses in case you think I am making this up.)

The gal was flying around the startled reptile's head, wrapping a piece of stout rope around its toothy snout as her husband grappled with the beast, all to the gasps and cheers of the onlookers. When the debris and dust settled, the 'gator was lying there trussed up like a hapless calf at a championship rodeo. It was then set in the boat and removed to a new location in the nearby Everglades, this after Jeff and I picked all the lures and flies off its hide.

Jeff and I ate all our meals for the next few days standing up; it was very uncomfortable to sit down.

Well, back to the culverts.

Culverts attract gamefish because culverts attract baitfish. Yes, this is the same principle that lies behind all structure. But culverts are especially productive because of the shadows they provide and how they act as highways upon which many fish travel. Tarpon (and jacks, redfish, and other gamefish) will take up positions near the mouth of a culvert to ambush baitfish as they come out.

Be very quiet when approaching a culvert; many provide quiet waters with fish that spook easily. Observe the water for a few minutes before making a cast, this to determine what fish are feeding where and to figure out where and how you should make your initial presentation.

Don't shy away from small culverts with little water to cast into. I have taken many nice fish from areas that appear to be home to only tiny mullet but which were in reality home to powerful silver kings.

ROCKY SHORELINES, SHOALS, AND THE SEAWEED CONNECTION

Maine's Seguin Island lies off the mouth of the Kennebec River, its granite shoreline draped in seaweed where countless periwinkles and mussels live. The Labrador Current bathes the coast of Maine with its chill waters and forms endless surges and waves that batter and wash up around the rock. In late May, Atlantic mackerel, also called tinker and Boston mackerel, arrive in the region and are quickly followed by extraordinary numbers of striped bass, the legendary gamefish now back from the brink of commercial and recreational overfishing coupled with habitat degradation and loss. (The striper was in good shape until the late 1970s and early 1980s when stocks suddenly plummeted because of this overfishing and severe habitat destruction in Chesapeake Bay, where 90 percent of Atlantic stripers are born.) Before the stripers deploy en masse, the mackerel can be taken on simple white or silvery flies all along the rocks of Seguin and thousands of other islands along the celebrated Maine coast. Fished within 40 feet or so of the shoreline, these flies (a Black Ghost with some Flashabou tied in to it is excellent) draw willing strikes from mackerel after mackerel, some weighing more than 2 pounds (called "jacks").

But shoreline structure to mackerel is not of critical importance. Yes, there is much life associated with seaweed-lined rocks, shoals, and shorelines here, but the mackerel are not dependent on these venues in this precise instance, although they certainly are in the big picture. They are merely passing by in search of the Atlantic herring and other shimmering baitfish that ply these cold waters. Herring do not hide amid the awash structure but rather swim in the more open water surrounding it, and the mackerel follow suit. Herring are found from the surface

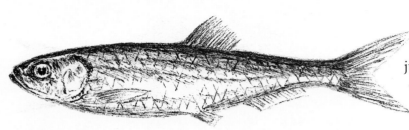

Atlantic Herring

to several hundred feet down into the gloom, where they feed on plankton, small shrimp, juvenile silversides, and even their own young.

So you see, sometimes structure can have only a peripheral effect on gamefish, and the angler who does not understand this goes home sad. On the other hand, when the stripers arrive in June, these rocks, shoals, and shorelines are crawling with them. What has changed? The mackerel have scattered by and large, so why are the stripers caught in such numbers so close to structure?

The answer lies in the forage. Mackerel do not orient intently on shoreline structure like rocks and shoals and neither do the Atlantic herring, but two other members of the herring family are often found very close to the shore and rocks. They are alewife and Atlantic menhaden.

First to arrive in the spring are the alewife, showing up in late April and growing in number well into May. At times these giant herring (they can attain lengths of 15 inches) can become so thick in the water at choke points such as the riffles below Warren village on the St. George River and in the Powder Mill Hole above the village that one can impale them with a pitchfork with ease from the bank. Unlike their little cousins, alewife are anadromous. (When their progeny depart the freshwater streams, rivers, lakes, and ponds in the fall, a feeding frenzy of stripers can occur at the river mouths, partic-ularly at night when the youngsters are near or on the surface; they tend to go deeper dur-ing the day. The shoreline at this time can be a fine place for catching stripers chasing baby alewife.)

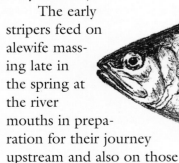

Atlantic Mackerel

The early stripers feed on alewife mass-ing late in the spring at the river mouths in prepa-ration for their journey upstream and also on those

Alewife

102

alewife that have already spawned and are returning to the ocean (alewife do not loiter once spawning is complete). When alewife return to the ocean, in fact as soon as they hit brackish water in many cases, they begin to feed heavily (they do not feed during the spawn). This feeding activity garners the attention of the early stripers, which charge the schools of alewife with abandon. But as the water warms and the alewife disappear, the menhaden arrive on the scene in staggering numbers, and menhaden often swim within spitting distance of shore and the surface structure it provides for so many things.

Atlantic Menhaden

This is the perfect opportunity to cast large (up to 4/0) Bunkers and Deceivers near any shoreline structure ("bunker" is a common nickname in the Northeast for menhaden, but along the Maine coast they are more commonly known as "pogies"). Flyfishers who study the tides and find favored locations of stripers near cuts and rips where the surface is energized with wave and current action will come home happy, their muscles pleasantly sore from repeated battles with strong striped bass.

In this instance we see that seasonal changes bring changes in the forage, and even though that forage is all related, as in the case of Atlantic herring, alewife, and Atlantic menhaden, the forage changes with the seasons.

JETTIES

Hundreds of miles to the south, the north jetty below Cape Canaveral at the inlet presents different shoreline structure. With a sand bottom, the water a few feet deep and jutting out into the surf zone, this jetty plays host to ladyfish, red drum, crevalle jack, spotted seatrout, sailor's choice, and other species. The rocks aren't covered with seaweed like those of New England and California, and the bottom is almost featureless, but these rocks composing the jetty nevertheless attract gamefish eligible for the fly.

Shrimp are the key. Florida waters hold shrimp throughout the year, and they are the primary forage at this jetty. Shrimp imitations like Bramblett's Swimming Shrimp and assorted patterns of Snapping Shrimp presented up close to the rocks and worked away from them at an angle or parallel to the structure will draw strike after strike, especially on the falling tide. The falling tide is almost always better than the flood tide at river mouths because the gamefish gather near the mouth to wait for the bait that is coming down from the hinterland. A spring flood tide is often the best of all because of the extra forage in the water caused by the higher than normal tide that has reached into areas left unmolested by less extreme tides.

Shrimp

I first fished this jetty in the early 1970s and soon learned that if you didn't have live shrimp, you weren't going to catch anywhere near as many fish as you would if you did. Yes, I was using spinning gear back then, not yet realizing that one could flyfish in saltwater. It wasn't until I read an article in *Salt Water Sportsman* by Mark Sosin and the writings of Lefty Kreh that I heard about saltwater flyfishing being in its infancy but available to anyone with a fly rod. This jetty represents a classic example of how the gamefish in one small area will heavily focus on one type of prey to the almost total exclusion of others. This isn't to say, however, that the drum near the jetty will always ignore a crab, because they often won't, but the fact remains that shrimp are first on the menu.

But things are different along the rock jetties of southern California. For example, behind the Hotel Del Coronado on the beach where I used to train lifeguards, there is a small rocky jetty. The water is shallow and the surf is filled with surfperch (barred, walleye, rainbow, black, calico, and others), halibut, and California corbina. All of these gamefish are fairly eclectic in their forage needs, but clamworms are a favorite. I discovered this by watching a spin fisherman cast clamworms into the surf beside the jetty and continually pull out halibut, surfperch, and corbina. When he left, I waded out beside the jetty with my swim goggles on and lifted up some of the smaller submerged rocks. Underneath the rocks were small holes, which I excavated with my hands while being pushed around by the incoming waves. In each hole, which averaged about a foot deep, was a green clamworm. (I wonder what the sunbathers and swimmers were thinking as the lifeguard trainer began rooting around under the rocks of the jetty.)

Standing knee-deep in the chilly water an hour later, after having retrieved my fly rod from the Jeep, I began casting the largest olive Woolly Bugger I had into the surf and was rewarded with three large barred surfperch, one fat corbina (an underrated gamefish in my opinion), and one halibut of about 5 pounds, all within 20 minutes.

Later that year (1985) I was in a Zodiac boat about midnight and noticed green clamworms swimming right on the surface here and there, apparently feeding, since they did not appear to be spawning. I returned the next night with a fly rod and had great fun sitting on a rescue board (a lifeguard's surfboard) catching corbina right on top.

But these fish will also readily jump on other flies that imitate other forage. The corbina and halibut, during the grunion run, can provide some amazing action. California grunion, which are members of the silverside family, spawn at night from about March (sometimes late February) to late summer. Starting two nights after a full or new moon and lasting a few days, the grunion invade California's many sandy beaches just before high tide and wash up onto the beach

Green Clamworm

with the surging waves. The halibut and corbina go mad at this time, and flyfishers willing to go out at night can experience great fun. A 3/0 Clouser or Deceiver in dark green over white or silver is all you need.

The longest jetty I fish is the Rockland breakwater, a massive finger of granite jutting out into the Maine city's harbor that is adorned with a lighthouse at the end, past which sails the ferry that plies the cold waters of the Gulf of Maine to Vinalhaven, North Haven, and Matinicus (pronounced *mah-tin-a-kiss.*) This jetty, and Rockland harbor in general, attracts mackerel and tommy cod that chase the silvery shoals of baitfish with seemingly endless appetites. The lowermost chunks of granite are awash with the tide and seaweed, and it is here that so many baitfish hide as best they can from the foraging prowlers. It is often easy to take the spunky mackerel and bottom-hugging tommy cod hereabouts, for the gamefish chase the bait up against this almost perfect barrier on a regular and very predictable basis. Linear shoreline structure like the Rockland breakwater is a tool for hungry gamefish, a tool that can just as easily be used by the flyfisher. And the chances of you being the only flyfisher on the breakwater are outstanding.

PILINGS

San Diego harbor is lined with pilings from near the mouth at Point Loma all the way back into South Bay near the Coronado Naval Amphibious Base and down toward Imperial Beach. These pilings run the gamut from the massive stanchions of the Coronado Bay Bridge and fat pilings supporting Navy piers at the naval station over at 32nd Street and the North Island Naval Air Station to narrow poles creaking beneath weathered docks. I first fished these pilings in 1984 and have spent countless hours in every nook and cranny of the harbor, and still I learn something new each time out.

Pilings, more than any one thing, are structure that hold fish very tightly, so much so that a calico bass holding on one piling will sometimes be unwilling to leave "his" piling to take a fly offered at the piling immediately beside it, even if the distance he would have to travel is only a few feet. Although in some cases the bass won't hit the fly next door because of poor visibility—low visibility is commonplace when fishing many pilings in salt water, especially cold salt water like that found off the West Coast and Northeast—I have found that calico bass and spotted sand bass are hesitant to leave their piling more than any other species, perhaps because they feel they might be risking losing their piece of structure to another bass if they surrender it, even for a moment. This is not true, however, of other

105

Concrete pilings often hold fewer fish than wooden pilings because of comparatively less marine growth on the concrete.

gamefish that might be near that structure, such as mackerel, which are only using the pilings in a transient way, more as neighborhoods to hunt in rather than homes to be jealously guarded. In the vernacular, perhaps these mackerel can be likened to drive-by shooters who cruise neighborhoods looking for likely victims instead of holing up in a house and taking shots at whoever happens to pass by.

What this means is that a fly must be presented to pilings in a very focused manner. Every piling must be hit, and on all sides too, if at all possible. This is important because in the dim water surrounding pilings, some gamefish tend to face in one direction, even when no current is running, and they may not be aware of the fly behind them or on the other side of the piling.

Although not true pilings, there exist in some waters bait barges, which are often anchored with cables and chains. San Diego Bay has such a bait barge, and the fishing around it can be nothing short of phenomenal. The chains or cables that hold it in place act like pilings and the deck of the barge acts like a floating dock. Flies worked adjacent to the barge and around the chains or cables can be devastating, especially when anchovies are schooling thereabouts. In eight hours on one summer day in 1987, Jeff Carothers and I caught 169 fish (not that we were counting) around this barge, the catch including kelp (calico) and spotted sand bass, mackerel, barracuda, halibut, and flounder, among other species.

Pilings can provide some of the most predictable saltwater shoreline action too. For instance, one afternoon in October of 1997, Richard Jee and I were fishing with Capt. Rodney Smith on the Banana River Lagoon. I mentioned to Rod that some jacks would be fun, and he didn't hesitate to bring us to a swing bridge over the lagoon, under which were many pilings that he said were home to lots of hungry jacks. No sooner had he said this when the water about 50 feet from the boat erupted in a great boil of foam, mangled mullet, and crashing jacks, which

were going about their business of dispensing mayhem like so many maniacal aquatic Cuisinarts. (I was very afraid.)

Pilings that are home to aggressive jacks.

Working these pilings required tough leaders (still, sometimes they weren't tough enough), the nerve to wait a moment before setting the hook, good boat handling (to drag the jack away from the pilings each time it ran for them), and the ability to put great pressure on the fish to turn it. We were eventually successful, but not before losing several fish. The jacks stayed around the pilings for perhaps 3 hours and then disappeared as fast as they had appeared.

OYSTER BEDS

The oyster beds between Mayport and St. Augustine, Florida, are some of the richest anywhere. Several summers ago I was fishing with guide and flyfishing writer Jon Cave and our friends with Suzuki Marine, Bear Advertising, Polar Craft, outdoor photographer Darrell Jones, and John Stamas of Stamas Yachts based in Tarpon Springs. I was on assignment at the time and was pleased to find that such notables as Jon Cave got that way because they pay attention and learn quickly, and then they turn around and readily teach others. Jon was no different.

Watching Jon work the oyster beds was a study in thoroughness. His effortless casts under all wind conditions and perfect placement and presentation were the stuff of years of experience. Something in particular I noticed was that Jon hit every oyster patch regardless of size, not just those obvious large beds that many flyfishers try. Even if there were only a handful of "blades" there, Jon's fly went to them.

Oyster beds are attractive to gamefish, notably redfish, not because the drum are eating the oysters but because of the other delectables drawn to them, such as the blue crab, which is often found in or very close to oyster beds.

107

The eastern oyster is the most common oyster from the Gulf of St. Lawrence into the Caribbean and down through the West Indies. It grows to 10 inches and has a notable ability to reproduce. This is the oyster we most often find growing in large beds and clustered onto rocks cleverly called "oyster rocks." Although it lives as deep as 40 feet, for our purposes in this chapter we are only interested in those growing in the intertidal zone and thus forming surface structure.

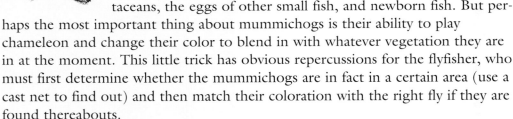

Mummichog

Eastern oysters grow in clumps that reach up toward the surface, their razor-sharp edges just itching to get at a leader or fly line or, better yet, the unprotected or poorly protected foot of a wading flyfisher. These rascals can cut through skin like the proverbial hot knife through butter, and cheap footwear is little protection. To make matters even more exciting, these oysters take on a brownish hue that camouflages them in dirty water.

There are two important baitfish that can be found in association with the eastern oyster, one often close to the bed and the other on sandy stretches in between beds. These are the mummichog and striped killifish respectively.

Actually, the mummichog is a killifish, too. It prefers the shallows and feeds around oyster beds that are growing within spartina or right beside it because it has a definite preference for aquatic vegetation where it apparently feels safer and is afforded plenty of its favorites to eat, such as mosquito larvae, tiny crustaceans, the eggs of other small fish, and newborn fish. But per-

Striped Killifish

haps the most important thing about mummichogs is their ability to play chameleon and change their color to blend in with whatever vegetation they are in at the moment. This little trick has obvious repercussions for the flyfisher, who must first determine whether the mummichogs are in fact in a certain area (use a cast net to find out) and then match their coloration with the right fly if they are found thereabouts.

From the brackish bayous of Louisiana to Texas you can find Gulf killifish, which are called minnows in some bait shops around Owl Bayou. My friend Fred Kluge, a very experienced and fanatical angler who lives between Shell Rock Landing and Parrot Swamp below Bogue Banks in North Carolina, taught me the importance of alligator minnows, the local name for striped killifish. My first lesson came just inside Bear Inlet, where there is a nice stretch of gently washed sand between oyster outcroppings. When there are but a few inches of gin-clear water on this flat, the striped killifish can be found and easily caught with a thin mesh cast net and then pounced on quickly before they wiggle through. A look at

Left: Jon Cave works the oysters.

Bottom left: An oyster bed north of Charleston at sunset.

these fish and you soon realize that a 2/0 Clouser—mostly light brown on top with a streak or two of black running lengthwise down the fish's center and a white underside—will likely do the trick quite nicely.

Fish the Clouser not in the 3 or 4 inches of water they are scurrying around in but precisely where the sandy flat drops off into the channel. A darting retrieve made perpendicular to the edge of the flat back toward the flat, and therefore imitating a striped killifish that is trying to regain the safety of the flat, will bring strikes from drum and specks as well as weakfish, small bluefish ("snapper blues"), and flounder.

109

SPARTINA

A type of cordgrass, spartina represents some of the most critical littoral habitat on the Eastern Seaboard from the mid-Atlantic to northern Florida and along the Gulf Coast. It is everywhere and everything to incalculable gamefish and baitfish. A day spent casting flies for redfish and spotted seatrout in the marvelous spartina marshes helping to form Little St. Simons Island on the south coast of Georgia is one of the most enlightening forays a flyfisher can undertake; an outing that you can make all the better, of course, should you be so fortunate to have secured accommodations at the wonderful Lodge on Little St. Simons Island (a fabulous lodge with few peers).

Much of what I know about the importance of spartina to the inshore marine ecosystems it helps define comes from Charleston fishing guide Capt. Richard Stuhr and Hilton Head guide Capt. Bramblett Bradham, two friends of mine who have kindly shared with me what appears to be an endless sea of knowledge stored in their salt-sprayed brain housing groups. Bramblett and Richard hunt red drum back in the wavering fields of spartina by poling through the stuff to small openings where drum forage for crabs and finger mullet. The flood tides provide just enough water to get the flats boats way back in to holes that most anglers don't even know exist. From their poling platforms over the stern, the duo can watch for tails and muds that tell of feeding reds.

It was Bramblett who first pointed out to me how rich an ecosystem a spartina marsh is. Staking the boat out, he reached down into the water and pulled up a few stalks of spartina. They were covered with tiny snails and other minuscule forms of marine life. Pointing into the clear water amid the stalks surrounding the boat, he drew my attention to the legion of crabs plodding and feeding along the fertile bottom. There were dozens of crabs in a single glance. I cupped my hands together and scooped up some water to get a close look at what I suspected would be an abundance of life barely big enough for the human eye to detect. Sure enough, the couple ounces of water in my hands were filled with life.

Tides are not radical in the South Carolina low country, nothing like those experienced along the Maine coast and those most extreme of tides found in the Bay of Fundy. The wealth of life in the spartina and the comparatively minor tides make life for the fiddler crab nearly perfect. Were it not for marauding redfish, the fiddler crab's existence might very well prove ideal. Fiddlers are creatures of the intertidal zone and can be seen in hordes at low tide when they come out of their burrows to feed in the mud. The mud flats seem to come alive as you walk along, as wave after wave of fiddlers scurry along the gray muck in front of you, waving their tiny claws about and gawking at you with stalked eyes.

Fiddler imitations fished on floating lines in the spartina openings and even

110

Above left: Capt. Richard Stuhr releases a tagged red drum back into the spartina.

Above right: Capt. Bramblett Bradham poles through a spartina marsh.

Left: Drum feeding in spartina will attack large baitfish like this white grunt as well as crustaceans and smaller baitfish like finger mullet.

111

right in the spartina where reds bulldoze their way through to get at the tasty morsels can be highly productive. Carl Richards' modified version of his black-tipped mud crab pattern is quite effective in imitating the red-jointed fiddler.

Fiddler Crab

Wading in spartina can be everything from okay to impossible, and a single marsh can give the angler everything from easy going to misery. The bottoms of spartina marshes, through which I have sloshed and attempted to slosh from North Carolina southward, are terribly inconsistent. Further, spartina marshes tend to have unexpected creeks running through them that, although narrow, are formed of the softest mud and prove to be hopeless in crossing and are often surprisingly deep. I discovered this in Mile Hammock Bay just north of North Carolina's New River Inlet several Septembers ago, and it is a lesson I shall always remember with considerable humiliation. My yellow Labrador, Rocky the Fly Rod Destroyer, was none too happy, either, and twice tried to bite me upon freeing himself from what was very nearly a retriever-eating stretch of mud.

But those same creeks can be excellent fishing as the tide falls. Position yourself off the mouth of the creek and watch the drum come down it as they abandon the now too shallow waters of the spartina marsh. They come along with that familiar hump or "push" of water in front of their big shoulders.

Silence is the order of the day when fishing spartina and the holes in the spartina in particular, where drum congregate and feed more easily on the exposed crabs. It is easy to "line" a drum or spook it with a stumble in the boat. And, of course, when one "blows out," all its friends in the hole follow suit in a great, sudden, mass exodus. When this happens, the hole is kaput.

Be especially watchful for the subtle signs available in the marsh, such as a few stalks of spartina moving when every other stalk in the marsh is perfectly still. A redfish might be rubbing up against it.

BEACHES

On my first trip to Cabo San Lucas one morning some time back, I stepped out onto my veranda at the Terra Sol condominiums and let my gaze wander down the empty beach. At the far end, near the giant cliff face that has obscenely large homes perched on it, were two anglers. They were catching sierras with the first rays of the sun—and catching quite a few at that—and the mackerel weren't small. Intrigued, I looked up and down the beach and saw not another soul, this despite the beach being quite long. Curious, I thought.

I walked downstairs and out onto the beach, the walk to the two gentlemen taking perhaps five minutes. From a polite distance I watched them catch several more sierras and then I headed back to the condo right along the steep, crashing waves. From my veranda I had seen plenty of structure in the clear water outside the surf zone, and now I was going to try to determine why the anglers were fishing where they were and not somewhere else on the beach.

I noted that there was a moderate rip tide with a cluster of rocks at the end where the two anglers were fishing. Walking back up the beach, I came to an identical situation in front of the condo complex. Being very familiar with rips and how they work, I watched as the water shoved up onto the beach was swept back out, taking with it many small baitfish that were plainly visible from the beach. Although I couldn't see them, I knew the sierras were waiting at the end of the rip where the strong current subsided. They were using the rip like a conveyor belt (an analogy that I know has been used in flyfishing books before, but which is most accurate), and the anglers at the other end of the beach were exploiting that fact. It reminded me of how beaches form structure that is point specific, meaning that the structure is often located in one localized area and that is where all the fish are.

Inlets

Many beaches have an inlet at one end, sometimes both ends. An inlet is as natural a fish attractor as there is, for it is like a funnel in that it squeezes a lot of water into a narrow space. That narrow space also squeezes a great many fish—game and bait—into the same narrow space, and this is where the flyfisher on the beach can have terrific action.

The dynamics of the inlet are important because the gamefish will not be spread evenly throughout. Instead, they will be found preying on baitfish from

Roosterfish and sierras are two prime targets near this rock at Cabo San Lucas.

ambush points along the edges of the inlet and where the seaward-rushing waters' power begins to wane. By positioning themselves at these strategic locations, the gamefish are able to attack the passing baitfish from a position of relative safety that allows them to conserve energy at the same time.

North Carolina's Bogue Inlet is a classic example. On the south side is Bear Island and a broad, exposed flat that is pounded by waves nearly all the time. There is excellent red drum fishing on this flat, but it is difficult to fish because of its exposed nature, although at low tide on a fairly calm day the flat is certainly fishable. On the north side of the inlet is the southern tip of Bogue Banks, which has a steep channel lip very close to shore. This side is fishable much more often than the south side, and there are plenty of fish to be caught there, too, with cobia (some surprisingly big ones that occasionally go into the 60-pound range), spotted seatrout, croaker, tarpon, Spanish mackerel, false albacore, bluefish (often many of them), and other worthwhile adversaries being a short cast from the sand. And just about where the current from the inlet subsides is a buoy marking the channel, around which you can find cobia on nearly every outgoing tide. The flyfisher who targets these edges and the terminus of the current can have a lot of fun with challenging fish.

One of the best forms of structure in an inlet is a buoy, especially for cobia. A technique I have used from Florida to North Carolina on visible cobia (the "man in the brown suit," as Mark Sosin puts it) holding on a buoy is the "suicidal bait-

The dynamics of an inlet.

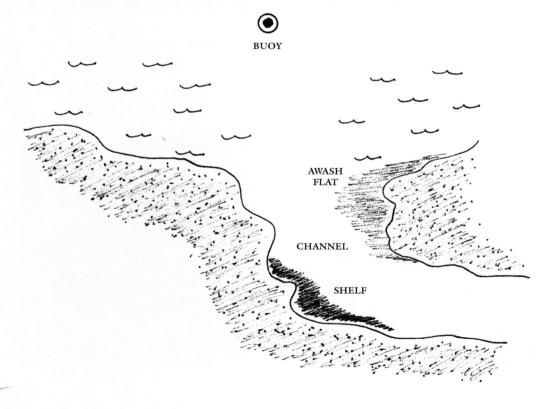

BUOY

AWASH FLAT

CHANNEL

SHELF

114

fish." You cast a large popper 10 or 12 feet in front of the cobia and rip it once on the surface. The cobia will orient itself to the noise it just heard and move toward the popper. When the cobia gets a few feet away, begin a rapid and steady retrieve that brings the popper right at and over the cobia. I have found that a cobia that sees this seldom fails to attack the fly. Yes, this is quite different from how you would fish to a tarpon, but it works.

Microstructure

Microstructure refers to tiny bits of structure—nooks and crannies—in the surf zone that attract fish. Every beach has microstructure, but it can be difficult to find without doing a hydrographic survey or flying over the beach in a plane at low altitude, which isn't a bad idea and is often very affordable (maybe $25 or so). Or you can learn how to read the beach, which is the preferred method.

Reading a beach is a matter of noticing the little things about the appearance of the water, including its color, action, and turbidity. A section of water that is brownish amid more blue water and appears slightly roiled as it moves faster back through the surf zone than the surrounding water indicates a rip current. A quick rule for identifying a rip is to stand on the dune (or the roof or hood of your vehicle) and look for what appears to be an aquatic path leading away from the beach out through the surf.

Note the submerged rocks below the nearest cliff face bracketing this northern California beach.

A confined area amid the surf that looks like a big boil tells where a rock or some other obstruction is, whereas bubbles and debris being swept parallel to the beach are an indication of an along-shore current.

Sometimes holes or minor depressions are created in the surf. These can be recognized by the slick or otherwise less choppy surface amid taller water.

Any form of structure in the surf zone is a good place to start your search. Also, watch for the usual signs of birds diving and baitfish scattering, and don't forget to look into the faces of waves, where baitfish and the predators chasing them can often be seen, especially if the waves are backlit and the water fairly clean (little sand being kicked up off of the bottom). Also be sure to watch for patches of slick water amid rougher water, which indicates a fish-oil slick caused by menhaden being attacked.

Breaker Bars

A breaker bar is a sand bar formed on the outer edge of the surf zone over which incoming waves crash and become breakers. Perhaps no more classic exam-

115

Birds can be marvelous indicators of fish . . .

. . . but sharp eyes can also spot baitfish in the face of a wave.

Right: Alcatraz.

Far right: Master saltwater flyfisherman Mark Sosin, rumors have it, learned to fly fish while "assigned" to the former penal colony. Mark denies this.

116

Hole or depression.

BEACH

ple of this exists than the breaker bars formed on North Carolina's Outer Banks, where behemoth red drum, toothy bluefish, and, once again, many large striped bass ("rockfish" thereabouts) bend many a rod.

The breaker bar attracts gamefish because of the many opportunities they are afforded to jump baitfish in the surf zone. Cuts in the breaker bar act as alleyways of sorts where baitfish attempt to run the gauntlet from the inner surf zone to the outer and back again. By standing on the dune or some other elevated point, one can see the cuts in the breaker bar with polarized sunglasses (I have a definite preference for Costa Del Mar sunglasses because they are 100 percent polarized and offer 100 percent ultraviolet protection), and it is often possible to see schools of finger mullet careening through the waves, especially if the wave is backlit with the sun first thing in the morning.

Breaker bars are often too far out for a cast from the beach. This is the time to get in the boat and cast toward the bar from seaward. Visibility is often very good in this situation, and sight casting to red and black drum, corbina, surfperch, stripers, blues, spotted seatrout, and the like can be very rewarding.

Saltwater shoreline structure, in all its forms, must be studied for its intricacies and nuances. Even structure formed by such infamous locales as Alcatraz in San Francisco Bay hold fish.

Remember that those intricacies and nuances mean knowing what is under the water even without seeing it, knowing what baitfish are likely to be there even when you can't see them, knowing what tackle you'll need, and being able to focus intently.

Rip current.

BEACH

Rock or other obstruction.

BEACH

Along-shore current.

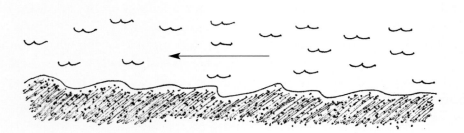

BEACH

Far left: As the tide falls away, you will know whether your estimate of the bottom was correct.

Left: This boil tells of structure below.

Middle: The author with a Belize River tarpon. (Peder Lund photo.)

Below: It doesn't look like much to the untrained eye, but this rocky shoreline at the Jaquish Gut at the end of Maine's Bailey Island offers excellent striper, Atlantic mackerel, and bluefish action to those who can decipher the rocks, waves, currents, tide, seaweed, forage, and weather, not to mention the fish you are after.

119

Chapter 7

Freshwater Shoreline Structure

Guide Taylor Streit prepares to net a trout for Pete Deison high in the Sangre de Cristos at Blackfire.

At an elevation of 8,800 feet in northern New Mexico's towering Sangre de Cristo Mountains, there sits along the South Fork of Coyote Creek a small ranch pond. Created many years ago when a rancher built an earthen dam on the creek and stocked with rainbow and cutthroat trout years after that, the little water is an excellent one for studying shoreline structure and its effect on trout.

I fished this pond at the Blackfire Flyfishing Guest Ranch near the town of Angel Fire for a couple of days over a Labor Day weekend and spent the entire time studying how the enormous trout went about their lives therein. Before making the first cast, I spent a little while interrogating Mickey and Maggie Greenwood, the proprietors of the ranch, on the history and ecology of the pond. I learned a lot.

The pond is very fertile with rich weed growth along the banks. Coontail, sedges, and spatterdock line the edges. There are no forage fish in the pond; the trout exist entirely on insect life. The deepest part of the pond is in front of the dam at about 25 feet.

Walking down to the pond and standing on the edge, I ignored the clown-like performance of what appeared to be an 8-pound rainbow leaping 3 feet out of the water out in the middle. Instead, I focused on the big cutthroat cruising slowly toward me along the coontail, sipping emergers that I couldn't see. Knowing that a caddis hatch might be imminent in the late afternoon, I tied on an emerger and flipped it in front of the trout.

Nothing doing. The arrogant fish glanced at my offering and moved along.

Shocked at this turn of events, I watched as the cutt went about its business. What I didn't see was the other cutt rapidly bearing down on my fly.

The tremendous splash of the take startled me, as did the wicked way my 5-weight rod was bending. Five minutes later and after a memorable fight, what was then the largest cutthroat I had ever caught was at my feet, waiting not so patiently for its photo to be taken.

But my mind was as much on the cutt that shrugged off my fly as it was on getting the photo right. Why did one ignore it and the other attack it as if it was the best meal it had seen in days? My best answer is that, frankly, trout are one of the few fish that can and always will remain somewhat of a mystery. But is there a hint that might help us solve the mystery? I believe so.

A MATTER OF FACTS

The Blackfire trout are very healthy fish living in a restricted, contained environment. The pond is small and the fish are big—much bigger than what is probably available in every other like water in the country, with few exceptions—and it is strictly catch and release, so the trout learn over the course of a summer that not all flies are what they seem. This is the hint. I suspect that the first trout turned me down because it had been fooled by that pattern before, whereas the second, more gullible or less experienced trout had not been exposed to that particular charlatan in that particular situation.

How then do we explain the big trout sipping flies in a scum line in a corner where the dam joins the eastern bank? I spied this fellow and the tiny dimples it was leaving just after sunset and quietly approached along the dam's face, which is lined with sedges. In the rapidly waning light I couldn't tell what it was eating, so I tied on a #14 bead-head Gold-ribbed Hare's Ear and put it 3 feet away from him. The fish instantly bolted from the scum line and inhaled the nymph. The 4-pound trout put up an impressive fight but eventually gave it up and allowed its picture to be taken. It was especially gratifying to see it swim away after a full 5 minutes of resuscitation.

This trout was using the dam as structure, with the scum line being produced by the dam where it formed a quiet corner of the pond. Although I doubt that my fly accurately imitated whatever it was the trout was eating in the scum line, I suspected that it would like what it saw as a substantial meal of opportunity

Pond trout depend on structure more than many flyfishers realize.

The dam itself.

123

and go for it. That particular fly is excellent when drifted several feet down all over the pond (a fact demonstrated time and again by Taylor Streit as he produced big trout after big trout for clients Pastor Pete Deison of Dallas and his thoughtful and kind wife, Harriet, so there was no reason for me to think that it would go ignored this time, this despite the trout having been focusing on a certain insect only seconds before).

CRUISERS AND THE VISION THING

Trout relating to structure in ponds are cruisers: they do not take up lies and wait for food to be brought to them, but rather go in search of food by cruising banks and the structure associated with those banks. Understanding the structure is the key to success.

Trout inhabiting ponds requiring them to cruise for food use more horizontal vision than those living in streams, the latter using more vertical vision because the food they are eating usually comes from in front of and above them. With 330 degrees of horizontal vision at their disposal, pond trout are superbly equipped to hunt on the prowl. Nevertheless, vertical vision is still important because even in a pond trouts' food is likely to be above them as well, only not nearly so often as right in front of them.

This point was driven home again and again at Blackfire, Gold Lake Mountain Resort, and Elktrout. Sight fishing is oftentimes easy in such places: the flyfisher can walk the bank and see trout cruising the bank and weed lines often within inches of the vegetation helping to form the shore. I decided to experiment a bit at Blackfire. Watching yet another large rainbow meandering along the bank ahead of me with its dorsal fin breaking the surface, I scooted forward of the fish and gently put a fly 10 feet ahead of but well off to its side. The fish did not see or hear the fly land on the water; I could tell this because it never altered its speed or course. When the trout was directly adjacent to the fly, I barely twitched it, the tiny ripple almost unnoticeable.

The trout instantly pivoted and rushed at the size 18 Parachute Adams, gulping it with no hesitation.

Intrigued, I took the experiment farther and performed it after the trout had passed the fly. The twitch came when the fish was actually 2 feet beyond the fly. As expected, the trout spun around and raced at the fly, attacking it with gusto.

So we see that shoreline structure and the pond it helps form can force a trout to adapt to the situation and in doing so break the rules, those being that trout feed almost entirely by looking forward and up as opposed to horizontally and barely up, and that trout will not venture far out of their way to take a meal. Structure can change a trout's ways.

124

Mickey advised me within minutes of my arrival at Blackfire that these trout must be fished slowly when along the edge. "Put the fly out there and just let it sit there," he said. "The hardest thing for people to learn here is fishing slowly. They want to go get the trout. If they would just wait and fish slowly, the trout will come to them."

ALL ASHORE WHO'S GOING ASHORE

Blackfire reminded me of another lesson learned long ago while walking through a field along the St. George River in Appleton, Maine. A grasshopper jumped up as I approached and was caught by the breeze and blown into an eddy formed by a cut bank. Less than a second later it was gone in a vigorous splash,

the fat brown making a quick and welcome meal of the hapless hopper. I wondered just how many grasshoppers that brown got to eat in a month, or a lifetime, for that matter. That was 1969.

Twenty-eight years later the lesson was again demonstrated, only this time thousands of miles to the west. A typical afternoon high-country thunderstorm had just blown out and the soft, golden sun of late afternoon was lending its warmth to the summer day. A grasshopper with a yellow body was blown into the water at the whim of a lingering breeze and was gone in an instant, an immense rainbow gobbling it with great energy. My mind flashed back to the hopper that fell prey to the brown long before, and an old suspicion seemed confirmed: trout voraciously eat more terrestrials than many people realize.

Confidently opening one of my fly boxes to retrieve a Joe's Hopper, I was mortified to find that I had left them all in my bass fly boxes in my den hundreds

Grasshopper imitations are fished too infrequently on most waters.

125

A Spent Blue Damselfy.

of miles to the north. I had but one hopper imitation and it didn't look anything like the one that had just been blown into the water. Would a size 12 Yellow Humpy suffice? Maybe. I tied one on and put it 30 feet away, a foot from shore. The question nagged at me: would color alone do the trick? I waited.

While waiting, I was chagrined that someone had apparently dropped a bowling ball from an airplane overhead, which landed right on my fly. No, wait! Another enormous trout had smashed what I had to offer and was none too pleased to learn it had been duped. Pleased as punch that color alone had come through, I stashed the lesson in the file marked "Close Enough" and shifted my attention to the damselflies cavorting around the shore vegetation.

I had noticed earlier that Greenwood's fly shop offered Spent Blue Damselflies. The insects these dry flies were actually imitating were bluet damselflies (*Enallagma civile*), some of the most common damselflies in North America. I had seldom used such large dry flies for trout but decided that, given the proliferation of these bugs all along the pond's shore, I had best give them a try, which I did the very next morning.

The coyotes woke me with their spine-tingling cries at dawn. Climbing out of bed and walking out onto the deck, I watched the resident elk herd grazing in the field above the lodge as I gave thought to the air temperature. Yes, I thought, just right. With the dew and chilly air, it might just work.

An experiment that I had devised the day before was to take some of the still wet-winged, and therefore immobile, bluets from their perches along the shafts of the sedges lining the bank and tossing them into the water. I grabbed my gear and headed down to the pond.

My legs were chilled from the dew clinging to the grass as I quietly walked along the west bank, but there, just where I knew they would be, were dozens of bluets. I snatched several of the delicate creatures from their perches and cruelly tossed them into the water. They floated on the surface, unable to free themselves from the grasp of the pond's surface tension.

Sitting down on a lichen-encrusted, volcanic (my college geology professor would want me to call it igneous) rock, I waited and watched as the pond awakened. First came the *wooosh* of a fine trout nailing something well out in the pond, and then came the rest of the gang working their neighborhoods for what-

126

ever looked promising and tasty. It wasn't long before I noticed a trout subtly working the sedges and coontail right in front of me, where the bluets twitched in frustration.

The trout—a dandy rainbow, and all of 18 inches—did not dash toward the first damselfly it saw but rather ambled over and sucked it down without any fanfare. It then slowly made its way to the others, sucking each down one by one and enjoying the easy meals.

Why wasn't the trout eating them more aggressively? I believe it is because the fish knew that once a cold and wet dragonfly fell into the water it was unlikely to get off the surface alive. The rainbow just didn't feel at all rushed. I dropped the mimic fly a few feet from the fish (no cast necessary; I just held the rod out over the sedges and dropped the fly down onto the water) and soon enough, over it came. It fought well.

The structure formed by the sedges and the chill mountain air, coupled with the dew on the damselflies' wings, added up to an easy trout that pushed 19 inches and was stunning in color, with bold, black spots along its dark back. In the solitude of the New Mexico morning, I enjoyed that rainbow greatly. So, we see that weather and the nature of each insect can play roles in determining how structure is approached.

But the casual way the trout went about eating the damselflies belies other situations. For instance, several years ago I was giving a catch-and-release demonstration in the trout pond of L.L. Bean's store in Freeport, Maine. This little pool is surrounded by large rocks, and a staircase winds its way up over the pond; the rocks and stairs were lined with people, and the fat brook trout in the pool seemed to know that something was about to happen because they darted back and forth waiting for the few handfuls of food pellets that they knew I was going to offer them. The grayish pellets are the only food the trout ever see and they like them, racing each other to get at the tender morsels first.

After I warmed them up by dropping several pellets into the water around me (I was in hip boots), I flipped into the water a special dry fly tied to look just like one of the pellets. Immediately a large brookie gulped it. I quickly brought the fish to the special catch-and-release net and released it with a hemostat in the proper fashion. The crowd applauded politely and the children were especially taken with the whole operation, pleased to see that the colorful trout was unharmed.

But why are these trout so ravenous and the trout of Blackfire usually so laid back?

The answer is simply competition. The L.L. Bean brookies eat only at certain times under very controlled conditions, and they live within the confines of a small pool. In contrast, the rainbows and cutts of Blackfire can eat whenever they like, for forage is always available in some form, and they obviously feel no stress from competitors. I watched two trout within a few feet of each other feeding on a mayfly hatch and neither trout went out of its way to beat the other to the punch; there was plenty to go around. Then again, when something special like a fat grasshopper or a larger-than-normal nymph appeared, they would tear after the morsel as if they were starving.

The moral? Every flyfishing scenario is situational, and one must be able to determine that situation and exploit all the factors of the structure being worked.

ROCKS

I would be hard pressed to make a guess as to which form of structure is responsible for producing more fish, rocks or vegetation. On the one hand you have spring creeks, lily pad beds, coontail, sargassum (technically an algae, as mentioned in Chapter 2), cabbage, sawgrass, spartina, water hyacinth, and the like, but on the other you have all the different types of rocks that everything from trout to snapper are attracted to, and these rocks come in an as equally diverse selection as vegetation. Then again, it doesn't really matter which holds more fish so long as you know how to work the structure.

The first fish I caught that was definitely oriented on a rock was a smallmouth bass on Maine's Crawford Lake in rural Washington County. I was casting poppers for smallies that were spawning in these absolutely beautiful waters, and the bass were holding among the big, gray granite boulders that adorn this wonderful lake's many coves. I was 10 years old.

The rocks of Crawford Lake were left there long ago by a glacier, and the

An isolated rock beneath an overhanging limb combines structure and shade, the perfect habitat.

lake is typical of this region, being oligotrophic for the most part but with a few areas being mesotrophic, the latter around the mouths of Huntley, Little Huntley, and Seavey brooks and the outlet to the East Machias River. Pickerel inhabit these mesotrophic stretches, with the bronzebacks having a definite preference for the oligotrophic coves and points.

During the spawn, smallmouths thresh out a nest in the gravel bottom of the lake in water between 3 and 10 feet or so deep. Their nests are quite visible to the naked eye even at maximum depth, appearing as circles of lighter-colored gravel. The gravel lies between the rocks, and the beds sometimes lie hard against a rock. Light-colored poppers, deer-hair bugs, and the classic Muddler Minnow all produce nicely, but a white popper with some black dots or stripes and a few white feathers sticking out the back is the preferred fly. The usual presentation is to make a cast beside or between some rocks and allow the popper to rest there until the rings of the bug's landing have dissipated. A twitch or chug may be all it takes to anger the male that is guarding the nest. It is nothing to catch all the smallies you want this way during early June.

Rocks along the shoreline that form fingers that jut out into the water, and those rocks that cast shadows and create little hollows, are prime suspects for lies. The presentation should be made with the fly landing first in front of the rock (between you and the rock) by perhaps 2 feet or so. This eliminates the possibility of frightening a fish holding on that rock by retrieving the fly from behind and past the fish; generally speaking, gamefish do not like flies coming from behind them. If no strike is obtained, cast again, this time putting the fly a foot closer to the rock. Continue this until something happens or it is apparent that there is no fish there or the fish that is there isn't going to feed. Also, if there is some water behind the rock, try a hook cast that puts the fly directly behind it, especially on the edge of a shadow.

Do not make the mistake of skipping the several feet of water between rocks lining the shoreline. Those open spaces can hold fish. Also, do not assume that the lies near shoreline rocks that appear less attractive to you will also appear less attractive to fish, because they might know something about that area that you don't, such as the fact that dragonfly nymphs are crawling around the fine gravel on the bottom there.

Finally, if you are coming up empty-handed on every shoreline rock you cast to, start changing flies. Go from a streamer to a large nymph, a popper to a wet fly, a Muddler to a Bunny Leech, or what have you. Keep changing and keep casting.

VEGETATED BANKS

These banks are the most common you will fish when it comes to freshwater shoreline structure on ponds and lakes. The vegetation can range from mature trees (and perhaps their roots) to lawn, and might include cattails, brush, over-hanging branches, and a wide array of other flora.

Fishing a vegetated bank is very situational. How you fish a bank consisting of cypress knees, trunks, roots, and stumps in Louisiana's Owl Bayou adjacent to Lake Maurepas might be completely different from the way you approach a bank lined with red pines on Minnesota's Woman Lake, a bank lined with brush on Maine's Sennebec Pond, or one lined with water hyacinth on Lake Okeechobee. All this calls for specific knowledge and tactics meant for a certain species or members of a certain family of fish. For example, a shiner imitation would be called for when working the sawgrass of the Everglades or the water hyacinth of a south Florida canal for largemouths, whereas a yellow perch imitation would come in handy if working the Crow Wing Lakes in north central Minnesota for pike. The banks of Lake Miramar in southern California would best be approached with a rainbow trout

Cattails are one form of bank vegetation among many.

This cutthroat came from a heavily vegetated ranch pond's bank.

130

A barely exposed rock bar in a former gravel pit.

These two anglers are working a bank in the Colorado Rockies for greenback cutts.

imitation if you are after the giant largemouths there, but you could use the same yellow perch imitation for pike in Maine's Belgrade Lakes that you used in Minnesota. A dragonfly imitation is good stuff on the gravel pits along Colorado's Front Range, but you would be better served with a shad imitation when after bass on Lake Moultrie north of Charleston.

ISLANDS AND EXPOSED BARS

Islands and exposed bars (rock or gravel) are natural attractors because they offer additional structure that tends to focus fish. Whether you are casting flies at the island just north of Great Pine Point on Maine's Crawford Lake, hitting a rock bar in Colorado's Sunset Pond, fishing a crawdad pattern in a channel beside a hammock in the Everglades, or trying to figure out the islands of B. Everett Jordan Lake in North Carolina, islands and bars produce more fish for flyfishers than we probably realize.

Casting flies at islands and bars is a game of niches and light penetration. The fish, regardless of species, are more likely to be concentrated in specific areas rather than all around the structure, and light penetration is likely to be a serious consideration. For example, there is a small island on Birch Lake in Minnesota across from the Shady Shores Resort. There are lily pads, logs, brush, rocks, and bulrushes around the edge of this island, but the fish are more often concentrated on the north side, where there is more structure and less light able to penetrate the water. A deer-hair bug for largemouths or a small panfish popper for bluegills fished on the north side is considerably more likely to bring a strike than the same flies on the south side of the island.

Chapter 8

Saltwater River Structure

Snags line the Mosquito Lagoon along Florida's Indian River.

T he structure of saltwater rivers could be said to be the most intricate of all waters, and it is this intricacy that affords so many gamefish such a bevy of places to feed and rest. It probably comes as no surprise, therefore, that most flyfishers never come to a full understanding of a saltwater river's structure. It doesn't have to be this way, but the fact is that most flyfishers simply don't spend enough time on a saltwater river to figure it out in its entirety. It is only time on the river, tremendous attention to detail, and a deep understanding of the river's flora, fauna, and cycles of life that make all the difference.

RODNEY'S 156-MILE-LONG LAGOON

Recently I stepped off the plane from Orlando, having just spent a couple of days in the company of Richard Jee and Capt. Rodney Smith, casting flies on the Indian River Lagoon, Mosquito Lagoon, and Banana River Lagoon. As you have probably figured out by now, Rodney is a respected, highly sought guide who fishes the complex waters around Cocoa Beach and Port Canaveral, Florida, whom I

Capt. Rodney Smith with a reasonable drum.

134

Left: Richard Jee fights a drum in the Mosquito Lagoon of the Indian River.

Below: Eric Davis, owner of the The Back Country, Inc. fly shop in Vero Beach, Florida, with a 40-pound tarpon taken on the North Fork of the Sebastian River. According to guide Bob Moore, this tributary of the Indian River may be the best juvenile tarpon fishery on the Florida mainland. (Rick Smith photo.)

first fished with some years ago on an educational New Year's Day. It didn't take long for me to see why Rodney was able to produce from the local waters the largest red drum ever caught on fly tackle for a client, and why he personally holds or has held IGFA tippet-class records. Rodney, you see, is a student of the river.

More a convoluted system of rivers, lagoons, coves, channels, creeks, canals, and flats than any one river, the Indian River Lagoon is 156 miles long and contains approximately 700 species of fish, some of which are revered by flyfishers— red and black drum, tarpon, ladyfish, crevalle jack, snook, spotted seatrout, and mangrove snapper, to name a handful. Although I had first fished this system in 1971, spending just a few minutes with Rodney reminded me that I am little more than a beginner in understanding it, for it takes a lifetime on this water to even begin to approach mastery of it. The remarkably diverse structure found there makes it all the more challenging.

With an average depth of about 3 feet, the fabled Indian River Lagoon and its related waters are a study in the abstruse. Adding to the hodgepodge of types of water are myriad forms of structure—mangroves, aquatic grasses (spartina, eel, turtle, and widgeon, for starters), dock pilings, buoys, rocks, logs, tree trunks, bridge abutments, channel lips, and countless others. So, with so many types of water in one system and with so much varied structure, one must choose his starting place well if he is ever to fathom the river. This is the time when a deep understanding of a gamefish's habits comes into play in a big way. Therefore, we had better begin on the shore and move toward the center of the river. And remember that although we are using the Indian River as an example, the principles that follow are applicable to many, if not most, saltwater rivers, and we will cite similarities along the way.

THE SHORELINE

Richard, Rodney, and I were working the Mosquito Lagoon on a bright, windy day, hoping to find some red drum. The going was tough; the drum were spread out and no schools could be found. The Mosquito Lagoon is part of the Indian River, which is now filled with baitfish since the 1995 inshore net ban in Florida went into effect, and Rodney was working hard to put us onto "his" fish. After coming up empty a ways south (closer to Titusville), we transited the Haulover Canal and began working the lagoon near Bird Island, where many brown and white pelicans rested in perfect order along the shoreline and where a lovely roseate spoonbill ogled us from a nearby black-mangrove.

Richard was standing on the bow platform with his 8-weight and a new Sage 5000 Series reel he was anxious to test. Rodney told us that the creek mouth we were approaching often held a drum or two and for Rich to be ready.

136

As we passed directly in front of the little creek's mouth, Rodney and I looked into the 2-foot-deep gin-clear water and saw the drum; two nice ones just sitting there 3 feet from the boat and for all the world appearing as if they were looking up at Rich and asking for a fly.

"Rich, drop the fly in! Those two fish are redfish!" Rodney whispered excitedly.

"They are?" Rich asked innocently. (This was Rich's first time after drum.)

"Yes!" Rodney and I rejoined.

Rich did as he was told and lowered the fly right in front of one of the drum, which promptly inhaled it and sat there waiting for something to happen.

"Hit him!" we both shouted to Rich.

Rich stripped in, the line tightened, and the drum bolted. The battle was joined.

There were several old snags right beside us, and the drum quickly headed into the nearest one. For some reason it didn't wrap Rich's leader around it and turned to come back out onto the flat—an amazing turn of events. Then it rushed the boat and caused much slack to appear, with Rich reeling furiously in response. The fish remained hooked.

Capt. Rodney Smith and Richard Jee with the unpredictable drum.

As have all newcomers to flyfishing for red drum, Rich made several more mistakes, but his luck held and after a while and a good fight, Rodney reached into the water and hoisted Rich's drum out. It was a handsome, coppery fish of about 7 pounds.

This tale is interesting for two reasons. One, Rodney knew that drum were quite likely to be at that little confluence; all gamefish are predictable to some degree. And two, sometimes fish that spook easily, like drum, do the strangest things, like not running from the boat that was a yard away, inhaling a ridiculously simple, almost ludicrous presentation, holding onto that fly until Rich strip-struck it, and then not breaking Rich off in the tree.

Let's examine reason number one.

Land Ho

Predicting what a gamefish will do, where it will be, and when it will be there to do just that is akin to predicting what a politician will say, when, and under what conditions; it oftentimes seems as though such a prediction is simply impossible. But the truth is that you can make what sometimes seem to be weirdly accurate predictions, provided that you are intimately familiar with the species in question. When it comes to saltwater river structure, this is where most flyfishers lose their way. Indeed, deciphering such intricate rivers as south Georgia's Altamaha near Little St. Simons Island (a privately owned island upon which sits the aforementioned Lodge on Little St. Simons Island) can be most challenging. Once you have cracked the code (made easier with the help of an Orvis-endorsed guide provided by the lodge), you will surely find yourself straining under the pressure applied by a large and stubborn redfish.

A long time ago, I found myself on Maine's ridiculously underfished Medomak River, just where the Hockomock Channel, Flying Passage, Back River Cove, Keane Neck, and the Narrows below Havener Ledge all form a convoluted confluence just north of Bremen Long Island, where Muscongus Bay takes a bite out of the rocky Maine coast. I was 16 years old and in a small boat with my girlfriend when I began to understand just how intricate a saltwater river is. (She dumped me shortly after this realization struck me; what can I say?)

We were catching dogfish (a species of small inshore shark) near a buoy, one after the other, and lots of mackerel and tommy cod in between, when it dawned on me that the lay of the land and the contours of the river's bottom dictated where and when the fish were feeding. When I revealed this discovery to her, she looked at me kind of funny; it wasn't long after that she discarded me for another fellow who was less interested in angling and how structure relates to

The inferior mouth of the red drum is perfect for foraging for crabs along the bottom.

it. Susan, the woman I eventually married, is more understanding, or at least tolerant.

But that day so long ago still lives in my memory, and from that recollection I have taken many fish in saltwater rivers. Saltwater rivers and how they are affected by the land they cut through and the shape of their bottom frequently confound flyfishers because they can't often determine what the bottom structure looks like, unlike many freshwater rivers which are clearer and shallower.

One answer to deciphering a saltwater river is to use a combination of attention to detail and deduction. For instance, the next major river north from the Medomak is the St. George (the Meduncook is a small river between the two), which greets the Gulf of Maine between the points formed by the town that takes its name from the river and Cushing. The St. George is a typical Maine river, replete with structure varied and abundant. Where the river turns at Thomaston harbor toward South Warren and loses perhaps 90 percent of its width, one can oftentimes find excellent striper and bluefish action, and this is possible because of the lay of the land surrounding the river there and the radical differences in the lay of the bottom. Let me explain.

Snook are very shore oriented. (Capt. Rodney Smith photo.)

The river is quite deep where it suddenly narrows beside the water treatment plant, but there is a broad, flat shelf just to the north where the river is still wide and where the "crick" (the Mill River, technically, but no one calls it that and fewer still even know its true name) enters the rivers. The edge of this flat, where the deep water joins the shallow, is formed by a lip of hard mud, which is excellent structure that has seen the tricking of many a blue and linesider. If you look at the land surrounding the flat, you see a gentle slope. If you look at the land surrounding the river's choke point at the harbor, you see much steeper grades. These terrain features are carried on into the river, and even a novice who has never fished here before, if he reads the lay of the land, can determine what the bottom structure probably looks like and tailor his approach from there.

Motor up the river a short way and you will pass through the narrows below the Maine State Prison. This is high-energy water when the tide is moving, and a legion of hidden rocks tell flyfishers to exercise considerable caution hereabouts.

Even when the tide is slack you can see thin seams on the surface that tell of the secret rocks below, and the flyfisher can deduct from there what he should do to get at the unseen stripers hiding in the dark water. The jumbled rocks and ledges of the shore and hinterland, if studied, also tell of what the river's bottom is likely to be made of.

So, we see that gamefish can be predicted by the lay of the land.

The Saddam Principle

Perhaps you were unaware that the actions of gamefish lurking in saltwater rivers and those of Iraqi President Saddam Hussein are both governed by the Saddam Principle, which even as I write this is confounding the leaders of the United Nations and several world leaders. These people really should flyfish more often; if they did, they wouldn't be having such a hard time figuring out and predicting the Buffoon of Baghdad, with whose so-called army I am personally acquainted, you might say.

The Saddam Principle states that predicting the unpredictable is impossible for those who don't flyfish. Richard Jee's drum didn't continue swimming into that tree because we expected it to do just that. Were we really ready for it to come blasting back out without wrapping Richard's leader around a limb? No, we weren't, and the fish was nearly lost because it didn't do as expected, with a lot of slack line suddenly making an appearance. For some reason, fish in saltwater rivers seem to do the unexpected more than gamefish in other waters. I don't know why this is.

If you are going to be fishing saltwater rivers, you had better learn to expect the unexpected. But what is it that makes these fish so predictably unpredictable? That question, I suspect, will remain unanswered for as long as we cast flies upon the water.

BRIDGE ABUTMENTS

One of the most common forms of structure on saltwater rivers is the bridge abutment. Abutments come in all shapes and sizes, and all hold fish, whether they are holding up a swing bridge on the Atlantic Intracoastal Waterway behind Onslow Beach, the Route 15 bridge over Eggemoggin Reach between Byard Point and Little Deer Isle, the Ocean Boulevard bridge at Long Beach, or one of many bridges throughout the Florida Keys. And all this is no secret, since anglers fishing from and under bridges are a common sight.

Bridge abutments can be similar to pilings in the way they hold fish tight. One of the most notorious gamefish found on southeastern bridge abutments (and pilings, of course) is the sheepshead, a type of porgy. Most fond of fiddler

The frayed leader tells the tale of the predictably unpredictable crevalle jack's way of rubbing against bridge abutments and pilings.

The devious sheepshead.

141

crabs, the scrappy sheepshead is seldom targeted by flyfishers, no doubt because other species perceived as more valuable (spotted seatrout, red drum, ladyfish, jacks, tarpon, snook, and the like) are being pursued instead. Another reason may be because the sheepshead is so deft at striking that most strikes are never felt.

The way around this is to fill a large clear jar with salt water and live fiddlers and suspend that jar by a length of heavy-duty monofilament near a bridge abutment; right up beside it is best, since the sheepshead doesn't like to leave his structure. Tie on your best crab pattern—author Jack Samson's Fighting Crab is tops—and fish it on a sinking or sink-tip line right up against the abutment. Now fish it with slow, steady strips that have the bare minimum of a pause in between. This gives the sheepshead the fewest opportunities to sneak a taste of the fly without being detected.

Many saltwater bridge abutments are swept with substantial current, which makes keeping a fly in the primary strike zone difficult. To counter this, use shorter, more accurate casts and make sure you fish every side of the abutment several times in case the fish on that abutment is on the side opposite your fly a few times. Weighted flies dropped right in beside the abutment can also be strong medicine. Shortening your leader as much as you dare also helps to keep the fly down.

The downstream side is going to hold fish more often than the upstream side, just as a rock in a stream is more likely to be occupied on the downstream side.

RIPRAP

Riprap consists of chunks of discarded concrete, cables, rocks, pipes, and other material placed in the water by man as junk. Riprap is where you find it; sometimes it holds fish and sometimes it doesn't.

Riprap, I have found, tends to hold fish that are more transient than those holding on larger structure. For instance, the swing bridge over the Atlantic Intracoastal Waterway at Onslow Beach in North Carolina has a section of riprap immediately to the north of the bridge beside the small pier. It consists of chunks of broken concrete and some cables. A steep channel lip lies 15 feet away, and many spotted seatrout are caught on that channel lip and on the shelf between the lip and the riprap, but only on occasion are trout caught actually within the riprap. However, if you walk 50 feet to the north, trout are caught adjacent to the riprap all the time, but here the bottom is a hard flat with almost no structure at all.

Why this is I have no idea. Perhaps the explanation is somehow linked to the unpredictable, for why would fish avoid structure and opt for a naked flat?

Riprap deserves your attention nonetheless, if only in the form of passing interest. But do be ready, because from time to time riprap on saltwater rivers can produce large fish, and often these fish show up most unexpectedly. I recall losing a very short battle with what I think was a big red drum in the riprap mentioned above. I wasn't ready for the fish when it slammed into my fly and emptied my reel in seconds. I had become unwary because I had been catching seatrout in the 2- to 4-pound range and just wasn't expecting something that weighed, I estimate, 30 pounds.

REINFORCED SHORELINES

Saltwater rivers are popular home sites, and many home owners reinforce their shoreline with rocks and even steel mesh netting to prevent erosion. Such structure can hold fish, although not often to the degree that pilings and bridge abutments do. Most fish holding on reinforced shorelines do so at the base of the structure rather than up along it.

Focus your attention, then, along the base of the structure with casts made parallel to it. A sinking line is useful here.

The ends of the structure often hold a few more fish than the center of the base. The sudden difference in the structure at its end seems to be what holds more fish; fish love anomalies.

For more information on saltwater river structure, please refer to Chapter 6 (Saltwater Shoreline Structure), which covers a lot of structure that is common to both a saltwater shoreline and that of a saltwater river.

Chapter 9

Freshwater Stream and River Structure

A classic Alaskan river scene. Note the salmon along this bank and the angler casting toward them from farther out in the stream. (Chuck Ash photo.)

On my way up to 12,000 feet in the Rockies—I won't tell you just where in the Rockies because of the extremely vulnerable situation the trout I am about to discuss have placed themselves in—to hit a high-country lake, I happened across a tiny creek perhaps 3 feet across. It ran behind a small stone chapel a cast's distance from the road and flowed into a small beaver pond.

Sneaking up on the stream, I peered over the edge and saw them: nine, maybe 10 greenback cutthroats holding in a little, crystalline pool no more than 10 inches deep. They were small trout, the largest perhaps 8 inches long. Swimming around them were some fingerlings.

I considered grabbing my rod from the truck and dropping a fly to them, but then I reconsidered. No, I would not fish for these rare trout, the road being simply too close for comfort, meaning that if anyone with a fly rod happened by at the time and saw me there with a rod in my hand, the secret would be out and the greenbacks would be the recipients of more pressure than they deserve. (All populations of greenback cutthroats are very susceptible to angling pressure.) Soon they would be gone. Better to leave them alone and be satisfied with just knowing they are there.

The greenbacks.

The structure of the pool is minimal. It has a hard sand bottom, gently sloping banks, and some willow saplings lining the south bank. Nothing else. As I spied on the delicate trout, one that I hadn't seen darted out from beneath the willows and grabbed some unseen meal on the surface, then disappeared back into the shadows. The roots of the willows barely formed any structure at all, really, merely forming a bank that is a bit rougher than the opposite bank. But this minuscule pool on a nameless creek and its subtle structure are all that the greenbacks need, and they may very well go unmolested there for some time, as they have apparently done for—how long?

And that is so often the name of the game in flyfishing a stream or river: subtlety. Of all waters, perhaps streams and rivers are the most perplexing when it comes to how to fish them when, and with what. Granted, many are easy marks with clearly defined structure lending themselves well to the flyfisher, but others are cryptic waters with fish well versed in the art of subterfuge and evasion. Therefore, let's examine the art of the stream.

THE ART OF THE STREAM

Let us begin our study of the art of the stream by examining the structure of the shoreline first, and then working our way out into the middle. For our purposes, we will use the word stream to refer to any body of water that moves down a gradient, which includes rivers, creeks, and like bodies of water. Streams are the quintessential flyfishing venue, of course, and their many mysteries have such an attraction that events such as the Chatsworth Angling Fair, which is held on the Duke of Devonshire's estate in Chatsworth each summer, attracts 27,000 anglers. Trout "beats" in the United Kingdom are, of course, where the foundation of our freshwater flyfishing knowledge was laid long ago. My family on my father's side is from Dartmouth in Devon, and my mother's side hails from County Kerry on the Emerald Isle. Perhaps this explains why I still thrill to the sight of a trout stream.

The stream is a place of energy, and it is from a keen understanding of this energy and how it affects a fish's relationship to structure that we are able

to deduce how and when to present our chosen fly to the fish. Failure to understand the stream's energy patterns will result in far fewer fish being brought to hand or net.

Top left: Energy is the key to life in a stream.

Top right: In a typical stretch of stream there may be dozens of lies.

Resistance Is Futile

If you have ever watched *Star Trek: The Next Generation* or *Star Trek: Voyager*, you are no doubt familiar with a species called the Borg. These part-humanoid/part-machine folks cruise around the galaxy "assimilating" other beings, and their favorite phrase to those they are about to assimilate is "resistance is futile," which is akin to a Marine sniper informing you that, if you run, you will only die tired. Naturally, Captains Picard and Janeway and their respective crews don't cotton to this assertion and always get the best of the Borg, this despite the Borg being apparently superior in every way.

Fish are to a stream as the *Enterprise* and *Voyager* crews are to the Borg—the fish win despite the seemingly overwhelming power of the stream. They do this by using the power of the stream to their advantage, which in this case is their hold-

147

ing in lies afforded them by structure within the stream. A lie is a refuge of sorts that allows the fish to feed while expending minimal energy holding its position.

A lie might consist of anything from a rock or log to a point or gravel bar, and it might be plainly obvious or very subtle. The trick is to learn how to read the water in such a way that the structure reveals itself and all its intricacies to such a degree that determining where the fish are holding becomes second nature.

This is made easier by first thinking in terms of needs. What does the brown in the Madison need? It needs a place in the river from which it can watch for food passing by while using as little energy as possible and which provides it with some semblance of perceived protection from predators.

Now switch gears and think in terms of physics. A brown is sleek and aerodynamic, quite like an aircraft; its body is shaped like a fuselage, its tail is used as an engine, and its fins, like wings, create lift. Commercial aircraft seek a flight level that allows them to maintain maximum efficiency; like an aircraft, the trout seeks a lie that allows it maximum efficiency, and it need not be a big or obvious lie at all. This last point is where many flyfishers miss the mark: they fail to realize what structure is appealing to the trout because they do not understand just how seemingly insignificant a usable lie can be. In short, they overlook the less than obvious.

Do not make the classic mistake of misunderstanding where a trout holding in a lie will take a fly passing overhead in relation to where his lie is. Trout in lies look forward and up, watching for meals on the surface (and also keeping a sharp eye out for meals tumbling along elsewhere in the water column, since most of what trout eat is taken below the surface). When a trout sees a meal floating above its head, it tips its pectoral fins up and rises upward as it drifts back with the current. It actually takes the fly downstream from its lie and then returns to it to await another meal. This is why it is important to present the fly far enough upstream so as to not spook the trout with too close a presentation. This also means that your ability to mend to get a drag-free drift and cast softly so that the line lands on the surface gently will usually have to be up to par.

TAKING IT TO THE BANK

Stream banks are as diverse as the streams themselves and consist of everything from rocks, thick brush, undercuts, fields, and gravel to sand, fallen trees, roots, lawns, and many other things. Banks are to streams as walls are to a room; they are critical to the health and wealth of the stream. Given this, we can correctly deduce that a large percentage of the fish in a stream are somewhere near the bank and are often using the bank as their primary structure.

As if to drive this point home, one day in June of 1987 I was fishing the

West Branch of the Penobscot between the Nesowadnehunk Deadwater and Big Ambejackmockamus Falls on a stretch called the Horserace. This portion of the West Branch is known for good salmon fishing, and I was anxious to try a new rod, so I careened through the woods to the river's bank.

The water looked excellent. There were several obvious lies perhaps 50 feet out and I began casting a Green Ghost. After more than a dozen retrieves through the best of these lies—or what I thought were the best—I began to doubt myself.

Taking some advice from a British friend of mine, Kevin Garner, who taught me that sitting down and having a cup of tea when the situation becomes a bit perplexing is strong medicine, I plopped down and contemplated the water. (I would have brewed some tea but was fresh out.) As I stared at the lies that had refused me, I nonchalantly flipped the streamer back and forth in the water at my feet.

The landlock that slammed into the fly hit with typical strength and vigor, startling me. The moment it attacked I knew where I had gone astray, realizing that I had been standing over the best structure the entire time. I brought the landlock in and carefully released it.

Top left: Regardless of size, the bank will play a crucial role in the lives of gamefish living in streams.

Top right: Salmon and Arctic char all relate to the banks of Alaskan rivers to some degree. (Chuck Ash photo.)

149

A few minutes later I was wading in an eddy when one of the largest brook trout I have ever seen—even bigger than the behemoths of Manitoba's God's River and along Labrador's western slope—took a fly less than a rod's length in front of me. The great fish rolled up onto the fly and inhaled it with a casual attitude reserved only for the biggest of the big. It appeared as though the trout had come out from under some sort of structure below the bank, which I couldn't see.

As I watched my friend, Bob Fant, fishing the river above me (a man who had spent 5 years languishing in the infamous Hanoi Hilton in North Vietnam after being blasted out of his Phantom jet in 1968), I contemplated how the banks of the West Branch were so important to the lives and livelihoods of the many fish therein. I noted the many other types of structure on the river, all of which seemed to be less important than that offered by the bank: pocketwater, logs, single boulders, deep pools, the Ripogenus Dam, slight depressions in the bottom. All were lesser digs.

But why are banks so significant?

The answer lies in the mind of the fish. Every fish in a stream has two concerns that override all others, except during the spawn: taking food without exposing itself to unnecessary risk and using as little energy as possible to secure that food. In contrast to other structure in the stream, the bank is more often the best place to achieve these goals. Let's look at why this is.

Safety While Feeding

It is common knowledge that the bank offers predators like the mink easy opportunities to catch fish, but those fish do not often make up anywhere near the majority of the biomass in a mink's stomach. This is much more often composed of muskrats (its favorite meal), snakes, frogs, small turtles, and mice. Most fish taken by mink (and those riparian comedians, river otters) are chubs, minnows, shiners, and other small rough fish, not trout, bass, salmon, and the like. Gamefish in a stream are much more vulnerable to ospreys and eagles, especially since the banning of DDT, which was getting into the food chain and thinning the egg shells of these birds of prey.

Mink

Baitfish, terrestrial insects (grasshoppers, crickets, ladybugs), and arachnids (spiders) are also more likely in many cases to be near the bank. The baitfish are near the bank because their instinct tells them that the major structure the bank represents will help hide them, even though birds like the belted kingfisher feed heavily near the bank. This phenomenon appears to be what the baitfish feel is a lesser-of-two-evils situation, in which they opt to run the risks associated with the bank rather than the exposure in the middle of the stream. Still, this seems to be one of nature's ways of providing forage for gamefish, because in reality the baitfish would be safer toward the open water, where fewer gamefish and predatory birds interested in hunting them are (wading birds, kingfishers, eagles, and ospreys). As for the insects and spiders, most are blown or inadvertently jump into the water near the bank.

The bank also affords gamefish a crucial safety measure in the form of shadow, of which the middle of the stream provides substantially less. Shadow is additional camouflage to gamefish, and they know how to use it very effectively. The vast majority of gamefish in fresh water seek shadows from which they can hide from those hunting them and pounce on those they are hunting.

Osprey

Energy Conservation

Because of the major effect the bank has on current speed, both in the broad sense and that of microcurrents, gamefish find that feeding while conserving energy is often easier near the bank where lies of all sorts exist, usually in larger numbers than those in midstream. Adding to this is the way forage seems to be continually swept toward the bank, as if the bank were some sort of prey magnet.

Even banks can mean little to the situation, such as when none of the forage being taken is terrestrial. (Chuck Ash photo.)

Streamers are a typical style of fly that often need only mimic action rather than a specific baitfish.

The shadow created by the larger of these boulders is a natural ambush point.

153

This event is similar to "ground effect," which is the pulling effect aircraft encounter as they pull out of a dive close to the ground, wherein it seems to the pilot as if the ground is sucking the plane down. Perhaps we can call it bank effect when applying the principle to flyfishing.

POCKETWATER

Pocketwater is that water which is quite shallow and covered with moving water that is inundated with rocks of various shapes and sizes. It represents some of the most challenging flyfishing, requiring short, accurate casts, with drifts being even shorter and customarily trickier to read a strike on when fishing a nymph. But pocketwater is a carnival of lies, making it a required stop on your foray.

Pocketwater demands slow, thorough, focused coverage. The chances of fish being in there are excellent, but you have to know how to work it.

On Maine's Rapid River, above Pond-in-the-River just upstream from the Chub Pool, is a stretch of typical pocketwater in which land-locks (the strongest and most aerially oriented landlocks I have found yet) and brookies reside. I first fished this pretty water back in the 1980s with George Misko and was instantly entranced with it; it spoke volumes without saying a word, for here were lies both many and disparate. Despite this apparent profusion of likely locales, it took me 3 hours of painstaking work to fool the first landlock, a racer that went perhaps 2 pounds that had fallen for, of all things, a size 16 Dark Hendrickson (as far from the traditional Maine landlocked salmon fly as one can get).

Bald Eagle

Why had it taken so long to manage that first salmon? I was being very quiet, which sometimes isn't extremely important in this high-energy water. I tried all the favorites, including Gray Ghosts, Kennebago Smelts (it was May and the smelt were swarming in the river), caddis pupae, Hornbergs, and various other offer-ings. My casts were short, and I covered every lie with attention to detail. So what was the problem?

My shirt. It was bright red. Looking back, I believe the salmon could see me because they were in shal-

Belted Kingfisher

154

Left: A rock bar, rocks, and a bit of pocketwater lend diversity to this stream, which often mean more fish.

Below: Typical pocketwater on a Rocky Mountain creek.

low, clear water (although it was highly oxygenated) and were probably nervous because of this. The final giveaway was when an osprey splashed into Horsechop Pool above my position and departed with a frantically wiggling brookie of a pound or so lodged in its talons. When I consider the lie I took the salmon from, I am even more sure of my hypothesis, as it was at the terminus of the longest cast I made in that pocketwater, where the salmon could not see me and my shirt. (Had this pocketwater been closer to the bank, I would have been able to mask my silhouette against the vegetation lining the bank, which would have helped disguise me; a tactic that is always advisable.)

One mistake in pocketwater and you will be disappointed, or at the very least frustrated.

I have found that most pocketwater is best fished on your knees with the shortest drop casts possible. Nymphs are probably responsible for more fish coming out of pocketwater than any other type of fly, so fish them heavily. Tight-line the nymph through each tiny pocket and be ready for the slightest change in your leader's action. If you think a fish may have taken your fly, it is probably already too late. Shades of Joseph Heller, I know.

POOLS

One of the first pools I ever fished was on a tiny, nameless stream that flows into Lowe Cove on Maine's St. Croix River above Passamaquoddy Bay, between the coastal villages of Robbinston and Red Beach. Nearly every day from the moment the alder buds were the size of mouse ears to the turning of the mountain ash and sugar maple under a brilliant and brisk autumn sky, I would leave my grandmother's house on Route 1 in Red Beach and head for the stream, stopping first at my great-grandmother's ancient farmhouse to partake of Grammy Lil's delicious peanut butter and molasses cookies.

From my perch above a little waterfall, I would dangle flies into the pool and catch exquisite brookies, none of which ever made 7 inches. I would marvel at their wonderful coloring and thought-provoking vermiculations and then drop them back into the pool. I haven't fished that stream since 1968, but the lessons I learned on it—and the pools on the nameless stream running out of Flowed Land Ponds below Carson Heath—I have brought along on my journey these past 30 years as I wandered from water to water on six continents; three decades that began with a lad in search of the truth and wisdom that only a brook trout can make known to a small boy—a future Marine, grandson of a soldier, and son of a sailor—growing up in the deep green shadows that secret the many mysteries of the Maine woods.

Great Blue Heron

Pools are the quintessential lie, for they offer to the gamefish everything it needs. When we think of flyfishing a stream, it is the pool that appears in our mind's eye, deep, dark, and still in the hushed shadows of a remote mountain valley somewhere north of nowhere. Yes, the pool is the foundation of the stream, and we must learn its secrets if we are to ever solve the riddle of the water.

Three natural lies in this small pool are 1) between the two small waterfalls, 2) in the shadow formed by the rock beside the upper waterfall, and 3) in the deeper water where the current flow from the waterfalls subsides.

The deeper water to the right of the larger boulder is an excellent hiding spot in this pool.

157

This dipper, having just exited the pool, is a good indication of nymphs in abundance.

The shadow near the bubble line in this pool is the place to drift a fly.

158

There is no need, however, to overcomplicate our study of the pool and how to fish it. At one time I thought that the pool was an enigma with no solution that could be applied to all, but over the years I have found that this just isn't the case. The point was driven home one afternoon on Minnesota's Cottonwood River near the farming community of Springfield.

The pool lies at the bottom of a steep bank lined with cottonwoods and it is quite typical of pools in this region of the upper Great Plains, with assorted rocks and a fairly soft bottom, the water slightly off color. I had never fished this pool before—hadn't even seen it before—and found myself studying it from the dark dirt bank.

Where would I be if I were a pike? A simple enough question.

I would be right over there between that fallen tree and the rock bar, that's where I'd be. And I would be there because an eddy is there where I can hide and wait with little effort for something to come by me, and I would be safe from attack, too.

There is no more to deciphering a pool than there is to figuring out any other part of a stream. It is a matter of deduction and a correct assessment of what the structure there has to offer a gamefish. There is no need to break the pool down into a dozen tiny subsections, each with its own name and special rules. Structure is structure, and the same rules apply to all. Energy conservation and safety while feeding are the gamefish's only concerns here, too. Find a place where they have both and you will probably find a fish.

I made a short cast to the pool and watched the leech imitation (a strip of rabbit fur dyed black with a touch of olive drab blended in) sink out of sight. I made one strip and the pike struck, surprising me, even though I had just chosen that eddy because it looked like a very good lie. A couple of minutes later I released the 18-inch northern back to its lair.

Why was I surprised? After all, I had intentionally targeted that lie after a study of the pool and knew pretty well that a pike was going to be in there. I was surprised because of how simple it was to observe the pool and deduce where the best lie was. I didn't stand there for an hour and think deep, philo-sophical thoughts about gradient, microcurrents, available light, forage possi-bilities, water temperature, turbidity, or anything else. I merely thought like a pike and made a cast with an obvious choice of flies to where my thoughts took me.

But, the truth be known, from time to time you are going to come across something unexpected in a pool, and perhaps even an unexpected pool itself.

George Misko and I had left Maine's white-pine- and paper-birch-lined streams for the sweetgum- and holly-lined banks of North Carolina waters in search of different fish. We had decided to give the upper White Oak River a go and felt that an exploration of the river above the confluences of the Brick Kiln Branch and Black Swamp Creek was in order, so we dropped George's Old Town canoe into the river just outside the town of Belgrade. Here the river is narrow, perhaps 15 feet in some places, the water clear and moving toward the fishing vil-lage of Swansboro at a surprisingly good clip for coastal North Carolina, a hap-penstance the result of a rare sudden dip in the earth's crust.

We hadn't gone 50 yards when we heard it. The river was about to change its tune and become a bit more rambunctious than expected. Wondering how we would get back up the river if we shot the rapids, we ran the bow into the bank, hopped out, and pulled the canoe ashore.

Discussing our options, we both noted that the pool we had just run through looked quite interesting, particularly the far bank, which was dark and brooding and had wax myrtle branches hanging over it.

"There's gotta be a fish in there," George said.

"Gotta be," I replied.

George had tied up some of his minuscule lead-head marabous and we both tied one on. They seemed to be the perfect solution to the demanding current in the pool. My first cast put the fly inches from the bank, and before the fly reached the unseen bottom my line tightened with surprising force.

"Damn, mister," George said. "That didn't take you long."

I was delighted with the fight the mystery fish was granting me, my 5-weight rod bending nicely with the collective strength of the fish and speed of the water. A full minute passed before my opponent finally gave up; a very big and saucy male bluegill with indigo sides and a bright orange-yellow belly. The fish was heavy with muscle developed from a life spent in a turbulent world.

George and I didn't even know that that pool existed until moments before that first bluegill, but a lifetime of flyfishing allowed us to quickly deduce where the best lie was. We employed the same assessment used to get the drop on small-ies in the St. George, steelhead on the Sol Duc, brookies in Orbeton Stream, browns in the Colorado, landlocks in Grand Lake Stream, and Atlantic salmon on the Ducktrap.

So it's all a piece of cake, eh? Well, no. The problem is that most pools have structure in them that you can't see, and many flyfishers have difficulty getting flies to go past structure they have no idea is there, which is understandable. And that hidden structure is oftentimes where the best fish hide, snickering to themselves about the oaf on the bank above and how he doesn't have a clue that they are even there.

What to do? The simplest solution is the one that takes the most time, but it is often effective, provided that you have the discipline and patience to see it through. I learned it back in the 1960s while watching my grandfather and father work a pool on the East Branch of Magurrewock Stream just east of the Moosehorn National Wildlife Refuge. So what is this secret?

Make sure you fish the entire pool from top to bottom.

Now that I have seen my way clear to bestow that wisdom upon you, let's see just how we can best go about this.

We must begin our exploration of the pool by considering what species are in it. What are some of the preferred prey species the gamefish in the pool like, and where in the pool is that gamefish most likely to be feeding on that prey?

In most cases the bottom of the pool is where most forage is taken. Obviously the bottom isn't the only place, since surface feeding activity is easily detected in a pool and nymphs swimming toward the surface to begin their new life are frequently taken before they make it, but the bottom is where the action is. And because the pool's bottom is often out of sight, we rarely get to see the myriad forage species that live there. This unseen world is why comparatively few flyfishers ever get to know what gets eaten and how down on the bottom of the pool. The result is their never having the opportunity to fish as thoroughly as they might have.

Right now you are probably thinking brown or rainbow trout, since I just spoke of nymphs, but the truth is that many gamefish eat nymphs with great rel-ish. Therefore, let's go just a bit against the grain and examine how to fish a pool for another species of equal merit.

In most waters, smallmouths take perhaps 90 percent of their forage under the surface and most of that from the bottom. Whereas in many waters crawdads account for a substantial percentage of this forage, they are by no means the only

Although craw-dad imitations for smallies are frequently pounced upon, crustaceans probably aren't the only forage the bass are eating.

or even the primary forage in most cases. Smallies also feed heavily on darters, sculpins, madtoms, hellgrammites, caddisfly larvae, leeches, and seemingly innumerable other creatures, so your work is certainly cut out for you.

This is an understatement, as it belies the complexity of the issue. For instance, it is a common misconception that all darters stick close to the bottom at all times. In reality, some don't. One example is the bluestripe darter (*Percina cymatotaenia*), which, although difficult to find in the first place, prefers to swim well off the bottom and even in the middle of the water column, and even prefers mud and sand bottoms to gravel runs, the latter of which most other darters prefer. Another misconception is that darters shy away from vegetation other than a handful that like emergent vegetation, but the dusky darter (*Percina sciera*) is commonly found in brush. And the saddleback darter (*Percina ouachitae*) goes against the grain by hiding in water so shallow that other darters probably think it is crazy; it hides in inches rather than feet, which makes it more vulnerable to attack from the belted kingfisher and great blue heron, among others.

But is the fact that there is abundant forage on the bottom the only reason why smallmouths and other bottom-oriented species feed there so often? No. Another part of the equation is the obstacle the bottom forms, an obstacle that gamefish use to trap prey against. The bottom effectively removes an entire dimension from a prey's bag of escape tricks; whereas a potential meal swimming well off the bottom can evade capture

Bluestripe Darter

by swimming up, away at an angle, or down, prey on the bottom can only attempt an exit at an angle or up.

Dusky Darter

Equipped with this knowledge, we must start at the tail of the pool and think three dimensionally. We want to cover the entire water column with casts that are likely to put the fly within view of the fish and make it appear to be something good to eat. And we have to do this intending to not miss a single potential lie in the pool. Most flyfishers can't say that they routinely cover pools so thoroughly. Can you?

Depending on the depth of the pool, you may need a full-sink, sink-tip, or even a floating line for the most shallow. Flies will be weighted or bead-heads.

Once you are ready, begin at the tail of the pool. You begin here because by doing so you stand less of a chance of spooking the fish holding toward the head of the pool. A fish being fought downstream of another is less likely to frighten that other fish. This is because the other fish can't see the one being fought without turning around, and far fewer vibrations given off by the hooked fish will reach the other fish.

Your first cast should be directed to a position that allows the fly to be worked right up against the very end of the pool's tail while also covering as much of the bottom as possible from the time it first settles down there. This means that you are going to have to avoid casts and retrieves that keep the fly down there only for a few strips; maximum bottom coverage on each cast is essential.

But what if the current is too strong? Mending isn't possible with a sinking line, making the densest line possible and the heaviest fly available a necessity. You must also be willing to make cast after cast to the same area if you suspect your fly just didn't cover all the bottom in the pool that needs to be covered.

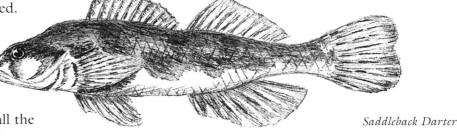

Saddleback Darter

Once you are satisfied that the first area has been covered fully, move up just a bit and cover the next in the same way. This is repeated all the way to the head of the pool.

Even on small pools you may spend half an hour working the bottom, and it may seem redundant at first, but you will take more fish this way.

REDDS

Not far below the tail race of Button Rock Dam on Colorado's North St. Vrain Creek there is a small pool just above where a culvert juts out from the bank. This morning (mid-December 1997) I was watching several trout in this pool's very clear water, the sun shining brightly and warming the 58-degree air. A minor chironomid hatch was going on at the moment, but the trout weren't especially interested in them, opting to feed on nymphs that I couldn't see but which they obviously could.

From my position on the bank above I watched what appeared to be the largest trout in the pool defend its redd (spawning site) from several smaller trout. In perhaps 10 inches of water near the tail of the pool, the redd was perhaps a 4-foot-by-4-foot oval amid an otherwise substantially darker bottom. Each time one of the smaller trout would encroach upon the digs of the larger, the larger would chase the interloper away and immediately return to its spot.

Although this redd was the only one I could see in the creek, the trout on it was adamant about putting off invaders. No doubt that had I cast a nymph so that it drifted over the redd, the trout would have had none of it. The midges hatching, however, were not perceived as a threat to the trout's territory and went ignored. One wiggled right on the surface and drifted directly over the redd, but the redd's owner just wasn't interested.

The trout can be seen here in the right-hand corner of the redd.

164

EDDIES

An eddy is a place of slack water that curves away from the direction of the stream's flow, often in a circular or semi-circular motion. Eddies are always suspect when it comes to lies, for an eddy is often the perfect ambush site where a trout can rest quietly and watch for forage passing right in front of its nose with little expenditure of energy.

The eddy in the photo below clearly shows the faster water going by the eddy's comparative quiet. But how should you present the fly? Cast directly across the current, forcing a quick mend to attain a natural drift? No; this makes the presentation unnecessarily difficult. Cross the stream and cast over the eddy? Certainly not; this will spook the trout by lining them. The best presentation will be made from downstream so that the fly drifts down the edge of the faster water beside the eddy. Be cautious not to allow your shadow to fall onto the eddy should you cross upstream of it. (Note: When wading and standing in the middle of a stream, watch for trout moving into position below you to eat the nymphs and scuds your feet dislodge. They will oftentimes gather quite close to you in small groups as they exploit the sudden forage boon you have created, which is a type of event drift, discussed later in this chapter. However, caution must be exercised when wading and dislodging forage. See my warning immediately following this chapter's section on tailwaters.)

A lovely classic eddy.

FOAM LINES

Foam lines are created by fast-moving or falling water and hopefully consist of air bubbles (as opposed to contaminants). The foam traps flies and holds them on the surface, making them easy prey for trout that know the deal.

Any time you see foam, get a fly into it, especially on the edges.

CONFLUENCES

Confluences—where two streams join or where a stream joins a lake or pond—attract fish because of the additional forage being brought into their ecosystem. Even seemingly insignificant confluences can be remarkably productive if fished correctly, and by correctly I mean thoroughly and carefully. Confluences are often more intricate and hold more fish than many flyfishers realize.

Above: Foam is to trout as fly paper is to flies. Exploit it.

Right: A foam line over deep water in a pool with shadows on both sides; an outstanding situation for the flyfisher.

166

This is a good example of a mountain stream confluence. If you were a trout, where would you be?

For example, the confluence in the photo above has formed a seam, two eddies, and riffles, all of which are attractive to fish. Most flyfishers, unfortunately, would focus first on the right-hand eddy and cast over the seam to get at it, thus spooking any fish holding in the seam. The best way to fish this confluence is first to study it and determine how you can work every one of its features without disturbing the fish holding in them. Begin by fishing the seam and then the right-hand eddy from a downstream position. From there fish the riffles while facing the incoming creek. Finally, hit the left-hand (upper) eddy (yes, you will have to mend a bit, but that is a skill you must master).

DEADWATERS

A deadwater is sometimes called a slick, usually with little obvious structure that would seem to have what it takes to hold fish. Such water is often passed up because of this apparent lack of structure, but in reality a deadwater can hold a surprisingly large number of fish. Deadwaters require close attention to detail, however, since the fish therein will be focused on structure hidden on the bottom and seams that are easy to overlook.

When I fish a deadwater, I tend to look first and foremost for the seams, which are created when slower water abuts faster water, and fish them from the bottom up, just like a pool. Seams appear as snakey lines on the surface and are

167

A deadwater on the North St. Vrain between Longmont Reservoir and Button Rock Reservoir.

attractive to fish because they allow the fish to hold in the slower water while looking into the faster water beside it, which brings more food past in a given period of time. The fish has the best of two worlds here, since it can watch for food while expending little energy.

To fish a deadwater seam properly you should make your casts perpendicular to the seam from the faster water. This approach allows you to keep the line off the water above the fish's head and therefore reduces the chance of frightening the fish by lining it. Your mending will have to be up to par in most cases when fishing dry flies along a seam, and when using sink-tips and full-sinks for wet flies, streamers, and nymphs, you will be making many more casts to ensure that you have covered the entire water column along the seam.

Deadwaters require stealth because they are places of quiet. Unless you take your time and try hard to be as silent as possible, you are going to spook fish that you aren't even aware of and will never see depart.

Deadwaters also have boils, many of which are subtle. Boils are created when water wells up around a piece of structure somewhere below. They are also approached from the perpendicular for the same reason as seams. When you can't see the depth of the structure causing the boil, you must fish from the top down to avoid a snag that will surely spook any fish holding on that structure. A high-stick drift with the line fairly taut is how to best do this. After the standard offers with a dry fly fail, get in tighter on the structure and begin working a nymph starting about a foot below the surface. Continue until you feel that you are just above the structure.

RIFFLES

Riffles are formed in thin water that is running over a uniform bottom with little blatant, heavy structure. They fool many people because to the untrained eye riffles don't seem able to hold large fish, or perhaps any fish at all, and therefore sometimes don't receive the attention they deserve.

Riffles are places of quick mends and careful study of the water, for most have subtle lies that are occupied by the largest fish. Any spot in a riffle that looks different from the surrounding water in any way has to be investigated. Often a depression as little as an inch deeper than the surrounding bottom is enough to hold a fish, and there will be some indication of that depression reflected in the appearance of the surface, which is often a slightly slick or less energetic appearance. This is precisely the case in the riffles just below the bridge where the Lincoln Pond Road crosses over the Kennebago River between Little Kennebago Lake and Kennebago Lake near the Maine village of Oquossoc. The thin riffles just above where the river bends hide slightly deeper water where brookies hold.

Many flyfishers walk right past this spot without casting a fly. George Misko, Bruce Busby, and I know better.

Dries, nymphs, and streamers can all be effective when working the riffles, although most flyfishers stick to dries and nymphs and opt not to try a streamer. I advise against always skipping the streamer because I have seen them work too many times in riffles to rule them out across the board. I once saw George take a nice landlock on a Green Ghost that he worked and worked and worked in some riffles on the Rapid River until finally the salmon he suspected was holding in a hard-to-see lie took it.

Naturally, begin at the bottom of the riffle and work up.

RUNS

Runs are stretches of water that are deeper than riffles, have a uniform, slightly ruffled appearance on the surface, and have current that is pretty uniform from bank to bank, although sometimes a slightly faster current within the run will be present. Pools aside, runs produce more fish than other types of water because they are obviously deep enough to hold plenty of fish and are often ease to access and wade. Visibility for the fish in a run is often good, making a quiet approach and efficient casts requisite. Mending is required, too, and you will have to be good at it if you want your presentation to appear natural. This is especially true when casting over a current that is faster than the one you are targeting with your fly.

(It just dawned on me that I have mentioned mending a few times in this chapter and haven't recommended a rod that mends especially well. Such a rod can really make a difference, too, and don't ever think that all rods are equal, particularly when it comes to so critical a skill as mending. After having fished with every major brand of fly rod, I find that I prefer a Scott STS for mending. This isn't to say that other brands don't offer excellent mending rods, because some do—Sage, Orvis, St. Croix, Elkhorn, and G. Loomis, for instance, all offer models of rods that mend well—but you bought this book for my opinion, so there it is.)

Runs are notorious for not being thoroughly fished because they are often long and wide. A haphazard approach will result in missed opportunities. Your patience level will be a factor in determining how you fish a run. For example, a patient flyfisher will fish a dry or nymph and spend hours on a run covering every square foot of water. On the other hand, a less-than-patient flyfisher will horse his way through the run using a streamer to cover water as quickly as possible or a dry fished on very short drifts. It's funny how, when fishing a run, the next stretch of water always looks just a little bit more enticing.

Left: Bruce Busby ties on a nymph to work a run on Maine's St. George River just above the Warren Village.

Above: Landlocked salmon frequent runs where smelt race upstream to spawn. This one was taken on Maine's Rapid River. (George Misko photo.)

Left: The author fights a large rainbow in a narrow spring creek run at Gold Lake Mountain Resort & Spa. (Court Dixon photo.)

Like pools, riffles, and runs, the approach is from the base of the run up to the next stretch.

I prefer to work runs by sections, selecting a piece of water for attention and working the fly into every crevice from surface to bottom until I am sure that every fish in that section has seen the fly. I will sometimes work the entire section again with a different fly if I feel that might be worthwhile.

THE MYSTERIOUS INVERTEBRATE DRIFTS

One of the most curious routine events that occur in a stream and that are related in one way to bottom structure is called the invertebrate drift, or more accurately, drifts, as there are actually three distinctly separate drifts. But in each case, a drift occurs when, for reasons that have yet to be absolutely proven—although some reasonable theories have been put forth, with one being probable—insect larvae and some amphipods (various scuds, of which there are 50 or so species in North America) leave the comparative safety of the bottom of the stream, swim up toward the surface as if they intended to emerge, but then stop short of the surface and simply drift downstream. I have found that those streams with more and longer riffles that have more nooks and crannies in the bottom have more intense drifts, which I feel can only be explained because of the additional minute hiding places in and on the bottom that offer substantially more cover for nymphs and scuds.

Here we should look at each drift, see how they relate to bottom structure, and examine how we can best exploit this peculiar yet often predictable occurrence.

The Event Drift

This drift, sometimes called the catastrophic drift, occurs in the spring when the ice and snow begin to melt and water levels and velocity rise. It can also occur when a thunderstorm or cloudburst upslope dumps a large amount of water into the stream in a short time, often only minutes. The spring runoff from melting snow loosens the grip of assorted nymphs and scuds and washes them downstream, where trout feed quite nonchalantly and rather unselectively on what forage comes their way. The trout are clearly aware that during this time the nymphs are not trying to emerge and the scuds are fairly helpless in the stream's increased velocity, and that since no particular hatch is about to occur they need not be selective in what they take; just about anything coming downstream is edible. This can make for fast fishing, as a wide variety of nymph and scud patterns can be productive at this time. (This is true of any drift.)

As a boy in rural Maine trying to grapple with the riddles of the local streams, I soon realized that late May and early June were excellent times to fish blackfly nymphs, but only on those streams that were well away from the caustic effects of pulp mills. (As a mere lad barely into double digits, I wasn't sure why this was at the time. I would learn later in life that blackflies, like brook trout, and to a somewhat lesser degree landlocked salmon, require very clean water to truly proliferate. The incessantly fuming pulp mills of paper companies, such as the malodorous, loathsome mills in the Maine town of Woodland and those along the Androscoggin River, were poisoning waters around them with impunity back then and in doing so were substantially reducing the population of brookies, landlocks, and blackflies. Maine produced 1.1 billion board feet of pine, spruce, and fir in 1996.) I would coat myself with Old Time Woodsman's Fly Dope (an evil-smelling concoction that was required by all Maine outdoorsmen come late spring down east) and fish the local waters—Quiggle, Fuller, Oyster, and Keene around Thomaston and Warren, and Eastern, Magurrewock, Rocky, Western, and the East Machias in Washington County—always finding as many brookies as I wanted.

The event drift didn't appear to occur at a particular time of day, either, so in the spring I knew I could find brookies—and a great many landlocks if I was fishing the East Machias below the dam at Crawford Lake, where, by the way, you are fairly unlikely to see another angler—at any time of day, especially on a warmer day when the ice and snow were melting more quickly.

Random (Occasional) Drift

The random or occasional drift is also likely to occur at any time of day or night, but the number of invertebrates in the drift is noticeably reduced. This drift also doesn't seem to last as long. Given this, the random drift is all but impossible to predict and more difficult to recognize. Most random drifts are unknowingly exploited by flyfishers who wonder why the past 10 minutes were so productive but for some reason the bite has now fallen off by 90 percent.

One sure way to tell whether the random drift is happening is to frequently use a seine while you are fishing. If your seine is coming up empty each time it is used in 2 hours' time, and then there are several nymphs and scuds for a short while, followed by their absence again, that is likely a random drift.

Behavioral Drift

This is the drift so many flyfishers are able to recognize and do something about. Occurring most often within a few minutes after sunset and just prior to sunrise, the behavioral drift involves caddis (except for cased caddis; *Ceraclea, Glossosoma, Brachycentrus*, and others; there are 1,200 species of caddis [*Trichoptera*] in North America represented in 143 genera), mayflies (except for burrowing mayflies—*Hexagenia, Ephemera*, and *Ephoron*—which see no reason to burrow out of the bottom only to place themselves in mortal peril), blackflies (*Diptera*), stoneflies (*Plecoptera*), and scuds (*Amphipoda*). But for the notable

173

exception of blackflies, midges (*Diptera*), which, like the scuds that are so important in Western streams and rivers, are generally not found in the drift.

Why this drift occurs is a matter of speculation, but some theories have been put forth, one of which is surely the most plausible and the only one I feel genuinely deserving of any discussion here. Most experts feel that the behavioral drift is nature's way of reducing the populations of aquatic insects at the larval stage. How else could such an occurrence be reasonably explained? The behavioral drift is virtually a suicide pact that occurs simultaneously among what, in some streams, are dozens of species across five orders all at once. They leave the safety of the bottom in their tiny hideouts and willingly head toward the surface with no intention of hatching, intending to be swept downstream where their instinct tells them death awaits.

The best time to fish the behavioral drift is, as previously mentioned, just after sunset and just before sunrise, but the middle of the night can sometimes be nearly as productive. This drift is very much affected by light penetration, and a bright moon can put the drift down. Check your calendar. When a new moon is present, the behavioral drift is often the best.

Do not restrict your fishing of the drift to trout. Smallmouths in New England feed heavily on the drift, primarily caddisflies, mayflies, and blackflies, and in the South they feed heavily on scuds. Landlocked salmon in northern New England and upstate New York also feed heavily during the drift.

OVERHANGS

Any structure that gives insects a place to crawl or land, and which is hanging over the water, is to be investigated. Limbs, branches, roots belonging to a blowdown, and other such structure are natural insect magnets. It doesn't matter whether you are fishing the many stumps of Florida's St. Johns River around Palatka, maple branches overhanging the Crow Wing River in north central Minnesota, alder leaves above the Salmon Falls River in eastern New Hampshire, or sagebrush along California's Lower Owens River, because flora along the banks of any river or stream can mean fish below. Sometimes very specific patterns are called for, such as the time I was fishing the Cimarron River below Eagle's Nest in northern New Mexico. There was a concentrated hatch of convergent ladybird beetles (*Hypodamia convergens*) taking place on a few bushes beside the river (here the river is much more akin to a stream), and the trout were feeding heavily on them. I watched from beside the bush as a flyfisher tried again and again to fool the trout with four caddis and six mayfly patterns, but to no avail. I told the man that the trout were eating the ladybugs and he asked, in a rather amusing tone, how I knew that. I told him they were falling into the water from the bush

174

I was standing behind. He stepped out of the river and came over to where I was standing to examine the bush, which now appeared to be alive with the tiny orange bugs. He didn't have anything that looked like the bugs, so I pulled out an Orange Scud, put a couple of black dots on it with my indelible marker, gave it to him, and told him to fish it as a dry. He proceeded to catch three nice trout. I left him to enjoy the hatch.

Be watchful for ants on the surface, too, especially on breezy days. Trout adore ants, even though they must have a bite to their taste because of their formic acid. When there are more than one species of ant on the surface, the trout can become rather selective, taking one species only. Always have a selection of ant patterns with you from spring through fall, including winged patterns.

So we see that even structure not actually in or on the water can still be quite important.

SPRING CREEKS

The spring creek is another thing altogether, as many a flyfisher will attest. Unlike freestone streams and well-known rivers like the South Platte, Big Thompson, and Kennebec, spring creeks are quite slow moving and are heavily vegetated. These two features are what make these creeks a challenge to fish.

Called chalkstreams in the United Kingdom, spring creeks are rich in insect forage. The abundance of aquatic vegetation in these creeks affords a tremendous variety of insects to live there, and the trout inhabiting spring creeks tailor their feeding habits to the reduced flow and level of forage. This means that you are likely to see trout feeding in a spring creek in ways that aren't the norm in more traditional waters. Naturally, you are going to have to adapt your approach accordingly.

Stealth and good eyes are what make the best spring creek flyfishers. These waters are quiet and the trout nervous and wary, so your approach and presentation must be equally subtle. Begin by observing the creek from well back and preferably crouched or kneeling so that your silhouette or shadow does not scatter the trout, most of which you will not be able to see (for every trout seen in a spring creek, there may be a dozen unseen but nearby). Watch for rising fish. With insect life abundant in the creek, the trout are often quite visible as they feed heavily. But wait. Rather than cast to the first trout you see rising, spend a few more minutes just watching. You are likely to see other trout rising that you hadn't noticed before, and one may be a better fish.

When you have selected the trout you wish to fish to, consider your approach, casting position, and presentation. Your approach to the casting position should be such that you can't be seen by the trout you have targeted nor the trout that you have yet to spot. If this means that you have to crawl or duck walk or slither into position, then so be it. Many trout are spooked because the flyfisher was too lazy to spend a few extra moments working into position.

Once in your casting position, recheck the position of the fish. If you can't see the trout right away, wait until it rises again. And check around for others; the angle at which you are now viewing the fish has changed and you may be able to see other trout which you don't want to spook or which may be better fish. Keep your false casts to a minimum so that your line or waving rod stands as little chance as possible of startling a trout. Your cast is likely to be best made from the kneeling position.

Accuracy and delicacy are important in the presentation. A botched cast that lands hard on the water is not good and will probably scare some trout. If you see that you should change your casting position because your drift is going to require too much mending, which could scare the trout, then work your way carefully into another position.

When the trout eats your fly, fight the urge to stand up. Instead, work the fish while remaining in the kneeling position. This is because many trout will only move a short way if bothered by a fighting fish nearby, whereas the silhouette or shadow of a human suddenly materializing on the bank will almost certainly put the fish down.

TAILWATERS

There is something of a love-hate relationship between the flyfisher and tailwater fisheries, which are fisheries below dams. The love side comes from the excellent fishing that can be produced because of a dam. The hate side comes from the unnatural and oftentimes destructive nature of a dam.

For example, one of the greatest tailwater fisheries is that of Lees Ferry, Arizona, below the Glen Canyon Dam, from which the Colorado River below Lake Powell erupts. Completed in 1963, construction having begun in 1956, Glen Canyon Dam, rearing up 710 feet and consisting of 10 million tons of concrete, resulted in the creation of a fabulous rainbow trout fishery in the 15.5 miles of crystal clear, cold river between the dam and Lees Ferry, where days of 20 to 30 large, strong rainbows are commonplace, with the trout averaging between 2 and 4 pounds and 5- to 8-pound trout being regularly taken. This dam has greatly improved the fishing in this part of the Colorado and is a good, albeit unnatural thing.

Another dam that sustains a good fishery is Maine's Ripogenus Dam on the West Branch of the Penobscot. The diverse waters below the dam offer good to sometimes excellent flyfishing for landlocked salmon and brook trout, and in doing so the dam helps support an important economic base for anglers, guides, and rafters.

On the other hand, many dams severely damage the environment and are responsible for the destruction of fisheries from coast to coast. The worst dams are those that block salmonid migration routes and prevent other anadromous species from reaching traditional spawning grounds. The utility companies that operate these dams have been astoundingly fierce foes when it comes to fending off those with environmental concerns, and the Federal Energy Regulatory Commission (FERC), which regulates dams, has been in the utility companies' back pockets since its inception. It wasn't until 1997 that FERC finally ordered a dam removed (the heinously destructive Edwards Dam on Maine's Kennebec River), but it remains to be seen whether the traditionally recalcitrant commission will follow suit with other deadly dams.

Inset: Lees Ferry guide Barbara Foster subduing a nice rainbow at Dam Island below Glen Canyon Dam.

Dave and Barbara Foster with a typical Lees Ferry rainbow.

Dave and Barbara's Tailwater Trout

I fished my first tailwater in 1968 on Maine's East Machias River, where a small dam at the Crawford Lake outlet sits. Landlocked salmon are the primary species to be caught here, although brookies are also present, and the landlocks are plentiful and usually willing. The latest tailwater fishery I have tried was Lees Ferry. In the interim I have come to learn much about these fisheries and have

Dave studies a glob of glomerata and finds annelids.

found that site-specific tactics as they pertain to each river's structure are critical to one's success. Let's examine Lees Ferry as a case in point.

Dave and Barbara Foster, Lees Ferry's top guides, are extremely knowledgeable of their fishery and can accurately expound on any topic pertaining to their river, ranging from geology and hydrology to aquatic biology at all levels, and they also have a keen understanding of all the tactics and techniques required to bend a fly rod. They earn their living by making sure that flyfishers who hire them wade away with the memories of many large rainbows caught (and released) that will last a lifetime.

The structure in the Colorado between Glen Canyon Dam and Lees Ferry runs the gamut from chutes, troughs, and classic eddies to flats behind gravel bars, riffles, bent pools, and runs. The bottom is mostly gravel, but there are some spots, such as at 8 Mile, where a sand bottom appears below the riffles. All this and the clear, cold, clean water, when added to constant water temperatures that are nearly perfect for rainbow trout (48 degrees Fahrenheit), has helped the river evolve into a midge-based fishery—more than 40 species of midges have been identified at Lees Ferry, which means that there are probably twice that number—

178

A rainbow holding in the shallows over a gravel bottom.

primarily made up of chironomids, although scuds (*Gammarus lacustris*) and segmented worms (annelids) are also an important type of forage.

Structure available one day may not be available the next because of fluctuating water levels, and Dave and Barbara have learned to play off this situation quite nicely. They point out that when the flow is increased, structure above the last high-water mark is flooded, which results in additional forage being made available to the trout. The duo made their point clear when we examined a glob of the river's primary aquatic flora, a filamentous green algae called *Cladophora glomerata*, which was available for examination at Dam Island just above the last high-water mark.

Dave noticed me taking macrophotographs of midges on a rock at the waterline and called me over to pull the *glomerata* apart. In the glob were several annelids, and other globs examined revealed *Gammarus lacustris* and assorted midge larvae. (Noticeably absent were caddis and mayflies, which are common on most other rivers in North America, and stoneflies, which are important on many Western rivers.) Newly flooded structure draws the trout into the shallows around it, where they feed heavily on the newly available forage. Dave and Barbara quickly focus on this new water.

Conversely, when water levels drop, the trout become more confined, which can result in many fish being taken from tight confines. It is commonplace to take a dozen or more rainbows within a 20-foot stretch of bank. I have taken approximately 25 nice rainbows in a 20-foot run beside Dam Island in 5 hours' time. I lost a 7- or 8-pound fish that performed an extended self-release after a 20-minute fight. It took me nearly 5 hours to hook that fish, too. (It was clearly visible for that time holding in a riffle in less than 1 foot of water.) Its early escape was quite disconcerting.

The author chasing the one that would eventually get away. (Ted Yost photo.)

(Perhaps I should note here that I mention numbers of fish caught only to demonstrate how many fish live in this stretch of the Colorado. I trust that you understand that the number of fish caught in a day isn't nearly as important as what you learned from each and the experience of catching individual fish.)

The structure of the river and its resulting trout and forage call for some very specific tackle and tactics. Extended-drift nymphing, which allows the fly to be seen by more trout on a single drift, can be accomplished two ways. One is by walking along the bank slightly upstream from the fly and maintaining a drag-free drift. The other is to mend the line and then shake some slack line free (either vertically or horizontally) to allow the fly to increase the length of its drag-free drift.

Rods used for nymphing should be fairly fast to handle split shot attached to the leader that will get the fly down to the right level, that being just off the bottom. Your favorite medium-action rod used for dries on rivers of moderate speed will be fine.

You will be mending on most casts, making a double-taper line nice if fishing light with a 3-weight, but a weight-forward floating line will serve you well on a more common and useful heavier rod and if you know how to mend well under varying conditions. (A 3-weight is considered by most guides at Lees Ferry to be too light for most situations. I agree.) Leaders are in the 4X to 6X range, 9 feet long for nymphing and 12 feet long for fishing dries. (Note: You may have to extend your leader beyond 9 feet when nymphing deep pools and runs to get your fly closer to the bottom.)

Flies are fairly simple. Nymphs should consist of midge larvae imitations, and

*Ted Yost does
battle with a
rainbow that fell
for a Glo-Bug
during the
spawn in Glen
Canyon above
Lees Ferry.*

Right: Deep runs might require a longer leader and additional split shot to get and keep your nymph just off of the bottom.

Below: In shallow water, be sure to remove any unnecessary split shot.

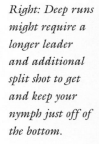

Right: The reward for having the right fly and knowing how to use it.

182

Top left: Dave uses both hands to fight a rainbow from the bank, avoiding redd damage.

Above: Richard Jee with a friend from Glen Canyon.

Left: The author nets a good Glen Canyon rainbow. (Richard Jee photo.)

183

Dave Foster's midge box shows diversity and a demented level of organization that surely won't be there for long.

184

The reward: a fat Glen Canyon rainbow.

scuds should accompany them in your vest or chest pack. Brassies in size 16 to 18 (occasionally 20), assorted chironomid midge larvae in size 16 to 24 (Zebras, red and silver, red and black), Hare's Ears in size 12 to 16, Pheasant Tails in size 14 to 18, and Prince nymphs in size 16 to 20 are all productive. Scuds are easily imitated with the Unbelievable, which consists of a "few tufts of orange poly yarn," according to Dave, who suggests fishing the simple fly along eddy lines and in riffles above gravel bars. Glo-Bugs in chartreuse, yellow, and orange, and brown Woolly Worms fished with a dropper below are good choices, with the Glo-Bugs being excellent during the winter spawn. San Juan Worms in size 10 to 16 (brown, red, and tan are best) mimic the annelids in the *glomerata*. Dries that can imitate clusters of midges are best during heavy hatches and include Griffith's Gnats, Humpies, Renegades, Grey Uglies, and Royal Wulffs in size 12 to 16.

A nymph dropper fished below a Glo-Bug during the spawn or a dry that mimics a midge cluster during a heavy hatch is a very effective technique.

When fighting a trout near a redd, leave the water if at all possible and fight the fish from the bank to avoid stepping on redds that may have freshly deposited eggs in them.

A NOTE ON SHUFFLING

Shuffling is a trick used to get trout to line up below your feet in a stream. In some states it is legal but others have forbidden it. Although I am unaware of

By slowing down and being meticulous in your approach, you will find that more fish come your way. This stretch of the Androscoggin River just below the Central Maine Power Dam between Topsham and Brunswick is excellent smallmouth water, but every crack and crevice must be worked for the best results.

any studies clearly showing that intentionally shuffling your feet in gravel or other bottom structure to break loose forage for trout is seriously harmful, it is best not to do it at all. The reasons you shouldn't are because it could harm important habitat and it could train trout to come to your feet, which is unnatural foraging activity. Besides, it is unsporting to shuffle up trout and then drop them a nymph. So please, avoid shuffling.

You will have noticed by now that it is of the utmost importance to work freshwater stream and river structure meticulously, being certain that every piece of structure receives attention. Flyfishers generally fish much too fast, which leaves untold fish never having seen their fly. If there is one rule for flyfishing freshwater stream and river structure, it is slow down.

Chapter 10

Final Thoughts

A day's flyfishing ends on a northern Minnesota lake.

U pon reviewing the previous nine chapters that account for a lifetime of flyfishing experience as it pertains to structure, I am struck by the fact that there is still so much more to learn and so many more ways to teach about the countless nuances of the water. Each time I take fly rod in hand and attempt to fool a fish, be it a Cabo San Lucas roosterfish, Maine smallmouth, California barracuda, western North Carolina brook trout, Molokai mahi mahi, Belize tarpon, Florida redfish, Colorado brown, Costa Rica bigeye trevally, or what have you, I still venture forth of a mind to learn something new or at least take a new angle at something learned long ago. I hope it remains this way forever.

Your journey, I suspect, will be similar to mine if you will only seek out the unexpected and challenging and be patient enough to stick to the longer path, which I have found to be much more interesting, enlightening, and rewarding than the short. There is much more water along the longer path, and many more fish to be tested. (Then again, it could be said that the fish are testing us.) Along the way, I hope you will never place yourself above other anglers who use inexpensive tackle and occasionally keep a fish for supper. Tackle certainly does not make the angler, and most definitely does not make the man, nor does one's desire to eat a fish from time to time.

If I could leave you with one principle in mind that, above all others, will make you a better flyfisher, it is that of stewardship. If our children are to have healthy waters to cast flies upon, we must rein in commercial fishing companies and depose the politicians who support this ruinous and ruthless industry. We must find ways to eliminate toxic agricultural runoff. We must gain control of the powerful and unbelievably annihilative timber industry. We must get the deadly commercial hog industry under control. We must remove useless, destructive dams. And we must put a stop to industrial polluters who, like the commercial fishing industry and corporate farming operations, buy hundreds of our politicians every year in order to have their bidding done.

If every flyfisher would show in some tangible way that he believes himself to be a steward of the environment, we would all benefit to an unimaginable degree. There would be more fish on structure if we all chipped in to care for our waters, and that's the best reason I can think of to be a conservationist. That way, we leave more fish for our children and our children's children, which is the best thing we can do for the future.

Selected
Bibliography

This selected bibliography is by no means all the books you should read, but it is a good place to start. They certainly don't represent my entire flyfishing library, which I began at the age of 5 years, but they were all useful to me in writing this book and all have something to offer every flyfisher.

Beck, Cathy. *Cathy Beck's Fly-Fishing Handbook*. New York: Lyons & Burford, 1996. Cathy is one of America's best known lady flyfishers. This book shows why. It is an excellent entry-level primer.

Earnhardt, Tom. *Fly Fishing the Tidewaters*. New York: The Lyons Press, 1994. Tom has been flyfishing in saltwater for many, many years, and has only recently decided to put some of his knowledge and experience to paper. His first book is truly top notch.

Foster, Dave. *The Lees Ferry Angling, Boating, & Historical Guide*. Marble Canyon, Ariz.: Marble Canyon Books, 1992.

Hafele, Rick and Scott Roederer. *An Angler's Guide to Aquatic Insects and Their Imitations for All North America*. Boulder, Colo.: Johnson Books, 1987.

Hughes, Dave. *Fly Fishing Basics*. Mechanicsburg, Penn.: Stackpole Books, 1994.

Kreh, Lefty. *Advanced Fly Fishing Techniques: Secrets of an Avid Fisherman*. New York: Delacorte Press, 1992. Any time Lefty speaks of flyfishing, people listen. Of all his writings, this book is his best. Lefty is certainly the dean of flyfishers. His casting and teaching ability, and his knowledge of gamefish, is truly unsurpassed.

Kreh, Lefty. *Fly Fishing in Salt Water*. New York: The Lyons Press, 1997

Livingston, A.D. *Bass on the Fly*. Camden, Maine: Ragged Mountain Press, 1994. A.D. Livingstone is one of our most insightful flyfishing writers. I know of no one who knows more about taking bass on the fly.

McClane, A.J. *McClane's Field Guide to Saltwater Fishes of North America*. New York: Henry Holt and Company, 1965. The late great A.J. McClane was *Field & Stream*'s fishing editor for many years. His astonishing knowledge of fish and their habits is unapproachable. He is sorely missed.

McClane, A.J. *McClane's Standard Fishing Encyclopedia and International Angling Guide*. New York: Holt, Rinehart and Winston, 1965. The bible. Read it.

Meade, Tom. *Essential Fly Fishing*. New York: Lyons & Burford, 1994.

Merwin, John. *The New American Trout Fishing*. New York: MacMillan, 1994. John Merwin is much more than a writer and flyfisherman. He is a historian, naturalist, and weaver of interesting stories, but most of all he is a teller of truths and teacher of the ways of trout. He is surely one of our very best flyfishing writers and is in the same class as Cathy Beck.

Newman, Bob. *The Complete Guide to Fly Fishing Maine*. Camden, Maine: Down East Books, 1993.

Newman, Bob. *Inshore Fishing the Carolinas' Coasts*. Asheboro, NC: Down Home Press, 1994.

Newman, Bob. *North American Fly-Fishing*. Birmingham: Menasha Ridge Press, 1998.

Page, Lawrence M. and Brooks M. Burr. Freshwater Fishes. Boston: Houghton Mifflin Company, 1991.

Pobst, Dick. *Trout Stream Insects: An Orvis Streamside Guide*. New York: Lyons & Burford, 1990.

Rosenbauer, Tom. *The Orvis Fly-Fishing Guide*. New York: Lyons & Burford, 1984.

Rosenbauer, Tom. *Prospecting for Trout*. New York: Dell Publishing, 1993.

Rosenbauer, Tom. *Reading Trout Streams*. New York: Nick Lyons Books, 1988. Tom's best work.

Sargeant, Frank. *The Redfish Book*. Lakeland, Flor.: Larsen's Outdoor Publishing, 1991.

Sargeant, Frank. *The Tarpon Book*. Lakeland, Flor.: Larsen's Outdoor Publishing, 1991.

Sosin, Mark and Lefty Kreh. *Practical Fishing Knots*. New York: The Lyons Press, 1991. Probably the only knot book you will ever need.

Sosin, Mark and Lefty Kreh. *Fishing the Flats*. New York: The Lyons Press, 1988. The world's two top flats pros teamed up for this book too. Everything you could possibly need to know about the flats is in this book. A landmark work.

Sosin, Mark. *Practical Saltwater Fly Fishing*. New York: The Lyons Press, 1989. This book really broke the ice and showed thousands of trout and bass fanatics that they can have even more fun casting flies in the salt.

Swisher, Doug and Carl Richards. *Emergers*. New York: Lyons & Burford, 1991.

Whitlock, Dave. *Dave Whitlock's Guide to Aquatic Trout Foods*. New York: The Lyons Press, 1992. Dave Whitlock's excellent treatise on what trout eat and why.

Woolner, Frank. *Trout Hunting*. New York: Winchester Press, 1977.

Index

INDEX